LINCOLN IN PHOTOGRAPHS
An Album of Every Known Pose

LINCOLN
IN PHOTOGRAPHS

An Album of Every Known Pose

By CHARLES HAMILTON
and LLOYD OSTENDORF

University of Oklahoma Press · *Norman*

BY CHARLES HAMILTON

Cry of the Thunderbird: The American Indian's Own Story (New York, 1950)
Men of the Underworld: The Professional Criminal's Own Story
(New York, 1952)
Braddock's Defeat (editor) (Norman, 1959)
Collecting Autographs and Manuscripts (Norman, 1961)
Lincoln in Photographs: An Album of Every Known Pose
(with Lloyd Ostendorf) (Norman, 1963)

BY LLOYD OSTENDORF

Mr. Lincoln Came to Dayton (Dayton, 1959)
Lincoln in Photographs: An Album of Every Known Pose
(with Charles Hamilton) (Norman, 1963)

FOR YOUNGER READERS

Picture Story of Abraham Lincoln (New York, 1962)

*The frontispiece is from a photograph by Mathew B.
Brady taken at Washington, D. C., on Friday, January
8, 1864. The tailpiece silhouette of an early cameraman
in action represents Mathew B. Brady and was drawn
by Lloyd Ostendorf.*

LIBRARY OF CONGRESS CATALOG CARD NUMBER: 62–16476
COPYRIGHT 1963 BY THE UNIVERSITY OF OKLAHOMA PRESS, PUBLISHING DIVISION OF THE UNIVERSITY.
MANUFACTURED IN THE U. S. A. FIRST EDITION.

TO THE DISTINGUISHED HISTORIAN
FREDERICK HILL MESERVE

CONTENTS

PREFACE

EVERY KNOWN PHOTOGRAPH of Lincoln is printed in this book. Some appear for the first time. Others are reproduced for the first time from the original glass negative or collodion plates, unretouched and uncropped. Supplementing the photographs are vivid word-pictures of Lincoln by those who knew him.

In the fourscore and eighteen years since his death, avid collectors have ransacked archives, attics, and antique shops in search of original Lincoln photographs. Each decade they find fewer. It seems doubtful that many more pictures will turn up. The pioneer works of Meserve are now out of date, and the pictorial biography of Lorant goes far afield from photography and does not include the most recent discoveries. There is an urgent need for a definitive book that will provide a close-up of Lincoln as the camera saw him—his likeness with no added touch.

Lincoln's face was the delight of photographers. He sat for thirty-one different cameramen on sixty-one occasions. Alexander Gardner took thirty pictures of him, more than any other photographer; Anthony Berger is second with thirteen; Brady is third with eleven. Preston Butler also took eleven photographs of Lincoln, but only three survive. Lincoln had his picture taken in seven states. Sixty-three photographs, over half of those known, were posed in Washington, D. C. Forty were taken in Springfield, Illinois.

There are 119 separate photographs of Lincoln—39 beardless, 80 with beard. Among them are 32 stereographic or three-dimensional views, over five times as many as were known a few years ago. Each group of stereographs (taken simultaneously with a two- or three- or four-lens camera) is considered as a single pose.

Six photographs of Lincoln are published for the first time in this volume; seven more make their initial appearance in book form. Still another half-dozen are reproduced for the first time in their original or uncropped state. Of the stereographic poses, 27 variants are here first printed. Also in this book are 108 unpublished photographs of people and places known intimately to Lincoln.

The smallest photograph of Lincoln measures about one-eighth of an inch in diameter, the largest about 18½ by 20⅜ inches. Only twenty-four pictures were taken out-of-doors. Ninety-four of the poses are seated. Twenty-four are standing, and one is recumbent in death. The likenesses taken before his first inauguration number fifty-three; those as President, sixty-six. Two portraits show Lincoln with a book at his fingertips; four show him with a book in his hand; thirteen show him with books at his elbow. There is only one close-up of him wearing spectacles. Many of the other pictures are enlarged, however, to show the details of his features.

There are two daguerreotypes, one tintype (or ferrotype), 12 ambrotypes, and 104 wet-plate collodion photographs. The daguerreotypes (on silvered copper) and the tintype (on thin black iron) gave only one portrait for each exposure. The ambrotypes (on glass, mounted against a dark background) sometimes served as negatives to make paper prints. The wet-plate or collodion method produced a negative glass plate from which any number of copies on paper could be turned out.

The collection of Lloyd Ostendorf, started more than a quarter of a century ago, is the basis for this volume. But the authors examined scores of historic collections, private and public, to make certain that no unique photograph, no variant, no especially fine impression, was overlooked.

New finds and new data make a fresh numbering of the photographs essential. The numerical arrangement is that of Ostendorf, but the Meserve numbers are also retained in the Chronological Sequence on pages 354 to 392. In a few cases, when positive contemporary evidence indicates that a still-missing photograph was taken, the facts about the lost picture are listed in the chronology, but no number is assigned to it.

From these pages emerges the most accurate physical portrayal of Lincoln we are likely to get. There are even times when a photograph gives us a glimpse of the man *behind* the face. Lincoln himself knew the value of his camera likenesses. To a portrait artist who had not met him, he wrote: "The next best thing . . . would be to carefully study a photograph."

Charles Hamilton
Lloyd Ostendorf

September 10, 1963

LINCOLN IN PHOTOGRAPHS
An Album of Every Known Pose

LINCOLN'S FACE: A PROLOGUE

HE SPOKE OF HIMSELF AS HOMELY, but in many ways he was handsome. There was an uncommon virility in his looks. Early photographs show a face toughened by frontier life, hard as a hickory knot. Its sheer, rugged power is appealing; but taken one by one, the features are unattractive. His hair is coarse and unkempt and his big ears stand out from behind high cheek-bones. His eyelids droop, the right lower than the left, at times giving him an appearance of cunning. The left eyeball wanders. On his right cheek is a very conspicuous mole. A small bump on the lower lip, visible in many of the photographs, puts a hint of a sneer on his tight lips.

Yet this face is an anomaly. Under the heavy eyelids is an alert glint with just a touch of humor. His eyes are at the same time cold and warm, penetrating and dreamy. The pursed thick lips, clenched with determination, seem always on the verge of a smile.

During the war years, successive photographs reveal not just the aging of his face but the growth of a spiritual power which supplants ambition. Toward the end, his features, weary and ready for sleep, show a sort of peace even when the sadness lies in dark pools under his eyes.

It is a wonderful face—a good face to look at and to study, for it has just enough mystery so that you can almost, but not quite, touch the man behind it!

Library of Congress O-1

THE FRONTIER LAWYER FROM SPRINGFIELD. This daguerreotype by N. H. Shepherd, Springfield, Illinois, 1846, is the earliest-known photograph of Abraham Lincoln, then congressman-elect from Illinois.

Library of Congress   Reversed O–1   Library of Congress

Mr. Lincoln and Mrs. Lincoln: Companion Daguerreotypes

THE FRONTIER LAWYER'S WIFE, a bride of four years, also posed for N. H. Shepherd, one of the first photographers in the village of Springfield.

In her unpublished memoirs, Mariah Vance, a part-time colored servant of the Lincolns, recalled that fifteen years later Mrs. Lincoln, standing with the President-elect, dusted the two portraits in their Springfield home and observed: "They are very precious to me, taken when we were young and so desperately in love. They will grace the walls of the White House."

Laughed Lincoln, "I trust that that grace never slips a peg and becomes dis-grace."

Half a century later Gibson Wilson Harris, once boardinghouse roommate of Shepherd and clerk in Lincoln's office, commented, "I feel confident I am not mistaken in recognizing the portrait [of Lincoln] as the work of my friend Shepherd, before whose camera I know Mr. Lincoln sat once or oftener."

Shepherd's advertisement in the *Sangamo Journal*, January, 1846.

5

THE FAMOUS "TOUSLED HAIR" POSE by Alexander Hesler,
Chicago, February 28, 1857.

IN THE WINTER OF 1857, Lincoln was in Chicago attending a lawsuit and campaigning for the new Republican party. Some of his attorney friends asked for a photograph. Lincoln had none. Possibly he had not faced a camera since Shepherd posed him in Springfield eleven years earlier.

"I don't know why you boys want such a homely face," said Lincoln. "I'm really not dressed up to have my picture taken."

Declared an eyewitness: "He went in Hesler's gallery with his hair in a tumble. . . . Hesler passed his hand twice through Mr. L's hair to get it away from his forehead."

Lincoln looked in a mirror, then combed his hair with his fingers. The result delighted his friends and amused Lincoln.

ALEXANDER HESLER
Lincoln's campaign photographer

Lincoln commented later: "A short time before my nomination [for U. S. senator], I was in Chicago. . . . A photographer of that city [Hesler] asked me to sit for a picture, and I did so. This coarse, rough hair of mine was in a particularly bad tousle at the time, and the picture presented me in all its fright. After my nomination, this being about the only picture of me there was, copies were struck to show those who had never seen me how I looked. One newsboy carried them around to sell, and had for his cry: 'Here's your likeness of Old Abe! Will look a good deal better when he gets his hair combed!' "

To James F. Babcock, Lincoln wrote that he considered Hesler's photograph "a very true one; though my wife and many others do not. My impression is that their objection arises from the disordered condition of the hair."

Illinois State Historical Library   O–3

THE TRAVELING LAWYER pictured in a circular ambrotype by Amon T. Joslin, Danville, Illinois, about May 27, 1857. Joslin's gallery, the first in Danville, was on the second floor of a building adjoining the Woodbury Drug Store, one of Lincoln's favorite hangouts. The original ambrotype is mounted in reverse in a velvet-lined case.

8

WHILE TRAVELING the circuit in 1857, often by buggy or on horseback, Lincoln attended court in Vermilion County, Illinois. Although an indifferent lawyer who lost as many cases as he won, he gained friends by his geniality and his humorous tales. One such friend lived in Danville and was the deputy sheriff of Vermilion County. His name was Thomas J. Hilyard, and it was for him that Joslin took this glass ambrotype.

Actual size, Reverse image   O–3

In 1934, Hilyard's son, William, then a ninety-year-old man, told how the circuit lawyer and his father had "passed a photograph gallery, and Mr. Lincoln suggested that they have their photographs taken and exchange them.

"When father returned [to his home at Ridgefarm, near Danville], after the term of court where he and Mr. Lincoln had exchanged photos, he showed the picture with great pride to his family and stated that at his death it was to be mine.

"On June 1, 1861, I enlisted in Company A, 25th Illinois Infantry. Father died while I was in the Army, and when I returned home in February, 1866, after my honorable discharge, I made inquiry for the coveted picture. My aunt gladly turned it over to me."

Although some historians have dated this photograph during the court session of November 13, 1859, and others have placed it as early as 1853, most authorities now believe it was taken on May 27, 1857.

HE POSES IN A BORROWED COAT for Samuel G. Alschuler,
Urbana, Illinois, April 25, 1858.

THE COAT BELONGED TO THE PHOTOGRAPHER, Samuel G. Alschuler, and Lincoln's arms extended through the sleeves "about a quarter of a yard."

Lincoln had agreed to pose for Alschuler, but when he showed up in his old linen duster, the cameraman lent him a velvet-collared jacket. A witness wrote later that Lincoln "was overcome with merriment" when the short coat "proved to be a bad misfit." In developing the portrait, Alschuler left his fingerprints near the bottom, visible as a series of weird arcs in this enlargement.

The original glass ambrotype was bought direct from Alschuler by W. H. Somers, a circuit-court clerk who knew and admired Lincoln. A photographic copy of the ambrotype was subsequently owned by Lincoln's fellow lawyer and biographer, Henry C. Whitney, who first met Lincoln in 1854 while traveling from Danville to Springfield. Whitney tells the story of the photographer's coat in *Life on the Circuit with Lincoln*.

Nearly three years later, Lincoln posed again for Alschuler, this time at the request of Whitney. The second sitting (O-40) is the last of the 1860 photographs and Lincoln's first with a beard.

George Eastman House, Rochester, N.Y.

AN EARLY DAGUERREOTYPIST
AND HIS CAMERA.

LINCOLN AT THE PHOTOGRAPHER'S: "You may make a good one, but never a pretty one!" (Lincoln to Tom Cridland, Dayton, 1859.)

Facing the camera was an ordeal, even for amiable Lincoln.

A century ago, before the invention of the instantaneous shutter, a sitting called for the subject to "freeze" for forty seconds or longer, head rigidly propped against a torturous metal bracket or "immobilizer" while the cameraman counted off the exposure. Any movement ruined the picture.

Of all early methods of photography, the most exacting to the sitter and the most perfect in its results was the daguerreotype. Only two original daguerreotypes of Lincoln exist (O-1 and O-6), both distinguished for clarity and brilliance.

Invented by Daguerre in 1839, the daguerreotype was the earliest type of photograph. It consisted of a silvered copper plate, highly polished and sensitized with iodine fumes, which, when exposed in the camera and washed with a solution of mercury, recorded the subject in reverse on a brilliant mirror-like surface. No duplicates could be made from the original daguerreotype unless it was copied by photography.

Lincoln generally sought any excuse to escape a sitting. To artist Charles A. Barry he cried out, "Don't fasten me into a chair!" Although an unwilling subject, Lincoln appreciated the skill of the daguerreotypists and other early cameramen who so accurately recorded his features.

Just before Lincoln went to the White House, Charles W. McClellan, a visitor in his Springfield home, saw Mrs. Lincoln come downstairs with an apron full of photographs.

"Father," she said to the President-elect, "I'm sick and tired of these. I'm going to throw them away."

"Oh, no, Mother, I wouldn't do that," replied Lincoln. "Someone may want them some day."

Lincoln's hair was unruly, and he apparently delighted in mussing it up for the camera. When he sat for Hesler in 1857, he had just left the barbershop, but he tousled his hair before reaching the studio. The photographer combed it, and Lincoln complained, "The boys down in Sangamon would never know me this way." Then he ran his fingers through it and quipped, "Now I've made a bird's nest of it again."

Mathew Brady recalled his first meeting with Lincoln: "When I got him before the camera I asked him if I might arrange his collar. 'Ah,' said Mr. Lincoln, 'I see you want to shorten my neck.'"

Photograph of Lincoln in case.
Most early daguerreotypes were preserved
under glass in ornate gutta-percha folding cases,
secured with brass clasps.

Ostendorf collection   Reversed O–28

13

Ostendorf collection   Variant O–5

HERE IS LINCOLN as he appeared in court on the day he won his most famous case. Defending Duff Armstrong against a murder-at-midnight charge, Lincoln produced an old almanac to show that the state's witness could not have seen Armstrong kill the victim because there was no moonlight.

After the acquittal, Lincoln was stopped in the street by Abraham Byers, an eighteen-year-old amateur photographer who had acquired his gallery in settlement of a debt. Recalled Byers: "Lincoln was attending court and boarded at the National Hotel, where I did. After dinner he stepped out on the street ahead of me. I caught up with him, as I went to my rooms, and said to him: 'Mr. Lincoln, I want you to go upstairs with me to my gallery; I wish to take an ambrotype of you.'

"He cast his eyes down on his old holland linen suit which had no semblance of starch in it, and said: 'These clothes are dirty and unfit for a picture.' But I insisted and he finally went with me."

When Byers took his picture, he used the process of ambrotyping, a method of photography which had supplanted the daguerreotype about 1856. The ambrotype was a collodion or wet-glass plate which, when developed and dried, could be used as a negative to produce an unlimited number of duplicate pictures on paper, or could become a positive likeness when mounted against a dark background. Unlike the daguerreotype, it was free from reflective glare.

Of the known photographs of Lincoln, twelve are ambrotypes. Byers took two ambrotypes of Lincoln, retaining one. It was not until 1895 that the second turned up, published by Ida Tarbell in *McClure's* magazine. The two photographs are so similar that they are here classified as a single pose. In 1947, Byers' widow willed her original to the University of Nebraska.

14

Ostendorf collection   O–5

AMBROTYPE BY ABRAHAM BYERS, Beardstown, Illinois, May 7, 1858.
Shown in original brass mat.

15

Ostendorf collection

THE LITTLE GIANT, Incumbent

Ostendorf collec

STEPHEN A. DOUGLAS. Age 45. Height 5'4'
Made 130 speeches. Traveled 5,277 miles.

THE BIG BATTLE FOR THE SENATE—

THE LINCOLN-DOUGLAS DEBATES

HARD, COMPACT, clever, and a seasoned campaigner, Douglas ran for re-election on the Democratic ticket against the leader of the new Republican party, Abraham Lincoln. The rail-splitter challenged his opponent to a series of debates. In seven dramatic meetings the contestants fenced, to the delight of huge crowds. Their physical disparity added to the sporting spectacle. Soon the whole nation listened as the two men dueled over the question of slavery. Douglas ended the campaign hoarse and exhausted; Lincoln, still fresh, finished with his tenor voice even stronger and clearer.

16

THE GIANT KILLER, Challenger

A SHREWD POLITICIAN, Lincoln made capital of his frontier background, riding cabooses or hay wagons to the debates. But beneath his rustic surface was a fierce intensity, revealed in the ambrotype taken by T. P. Pearson at Macomb, Illinois, five days after the first debate at Ottawa. Early on Thursday morning, August 26, 1858, Lincoln went with James K. Magie to Pearson's gallery. Offered a mirror so that he could "fix up," he declined, adding: "It would not be much of a likeness if I fixed up any."

The full-length photograph on the right, a study of Lincoln's powerful physique, was taken at Springfield in 1860 by an unknown photographer for use by the sculptor Henry Kirke Brown, among whose effects it was found in 1931.

Library of Congress

ABRAHAM LINCOLN. Age 49. Height 6′4″. Made 63 speeches. Traveled 4,350 miles.

TOUGH CAMPAIGNER FOR THE SENATE. Daguerreotype by Polycarp Von Schneidau, Chicago, Illinois, July 11, 1858.

This portrait recalls Lincoln's witticism that his hair "had a way of getting up as far as possible in the world."

THERE IS A LOOK OF CRAFTINESS in the half-closed eyes and the slightly twisted lips, as though the campaigner had just scored a clever point. This is the intellectual Lincoln, his features alert and intense and his mind sharpened by the clash with Douglas.

Journalist Martin P. S. Rindlaub, who heard Lincoln debate at Freeport, Illinois, on August 27, 1858, remembered many years later that the tall candidate "was swarthy as an Indian, with wiry, jet-black hair, which was usually in an unkempt condition. He wore no beard, and his face was almost grotesquely square, with high cheek bones. His eyes were bright, keen, and a luminous gray color, though his eyebrows were black like his hair. His figure was gaunt, slender and slightly bent. He was clad in a rusty-black Prince Albert coat with somewhat abbreviated sleeves. His black trousers, too, were so short that they gave an appearance of exaggerated size to his feet. He wore a high stove-pipe hat, somewhat the worse for wear, and he carried a gray woolen shawl . . . ."

On Friday, July 9, 1858, Lincoln listened to Douglas lash out at him; on the following day he lashed back. On Sunday, July 11, he joined Isaac N. Arnold and George Schneider for dinner, and later the three men strolled down Lake Street, passing the old daguerrean gallery.

At the suggestion of Schneider, then editor of an antislavery newspaper, the *Staat Zeitung*, Lincoln posed for Schneider's friend, Von Schneidau. In his hands he held a copy of the *Chicago Press and Tribune*, a paper friendly to his ideas.

The original daguerreotype was treasured by Schneider until his death.

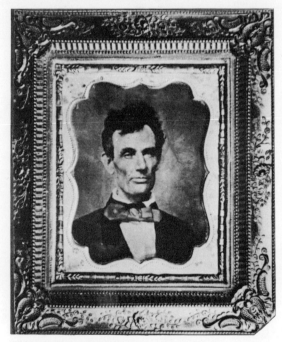

Chicago Historical Society   Variant O–6

"UNCLE ABE" POSES FOR A RELATIVE in this photograph, probably by C. S. German of Springfield, Illinois, about September 23, 1858.

Two days before his sixth debate with Douglas, Lincoln spoke at Monmouth for three hours. The lean, picturesque lawyer from the backwoods was now a national figure. This ambrotype was taken by William Judkins Thompson on Monday, October 11, 1858, while Lincoln was in Monmouth. Several days later the humorist Petroleum V. Nasby (David R. Locke) met Lincoln at Quincy, recording: "I never saw a more thoughtful face. I never saw a more dignified face. I never saw so sad a face."

Meserve collection O–11

◄ "This is not a very good-looking picture," wrote Lincoln to the granddaughter of his stepmother, "but it's the best that could be produced from the poor subject."

Taken by special request, as were most of his early photographs, this formal pose was made for Mrs. Harriet Chapman, granddaughter of Sarah Bush Lincoln. While in Charleston for the fourth debate with Douglas, Lincoln spent the night with A. H. Chapman, son-in-law of Dennis Hanks.

Just before he left, Mrs. Chapman said to him, "Uncle Abe, I want a picture of you."

"Well, Harriet," answered Lincoln, "when I get home I will have one taken and sent to you."

Describing the incident, Mrs. Chapman's son, R. N. Chapman, wrote to Ida M. Tarbell: "Soon after, mother received from Springfield, already framed, the photograph she still has with a letter from Mr. Lincoln."

O–10

22

THE CAMPAIGN FOR THE SENATE IN FULL SWING, Lincoln spoke in the Pittsfield town square for several hours. At the request of attorney D. H. Gilmer, who wanted a portrait of him, Lincoln posed for this ambrotype by Calvin Jackson (O–10), Pittsfield, Illinois, Friday, October 1, 1858, published here by courtesy of The Lincoln Memorial University.

The lines in Lincoln's face, plainly visible in this portrait, were noted by his intimate friend Joshua F. Speed, who wrote: "His face and forehead were wrinkled even in his youth. They deepened in age, 'as streams their channels deeper wear.' Generally he was a very sad man, and his countenance indicated it."

During his first campaign for the Presidency, Lincoln was visited by a gentleman from Massachusetts who noticed an unfinished portrait of the candidate by Thomas Hicks. "I suppose," he observed, "you have to give a good deal of your time to posing." "No," answered Lincoln, "this is the first time that I have had this specific sort of picture made, but I have had the sun pictures made several times." On the office wall was hanging a very dark photograph with a light background, and his guest said, "I see a photograph of you there, but it does not appear to have any sun in it." Lincoln smiled. "Parson Brownlow says I am a nigger; and if he had judged alone from that picture, he would have had some ground for his assertion."

HE LOOKS BLAND IN THIS FADED AMBROTYPE (O–7) by Preston Butler, Spring-
field, Illinois, about July, 1858. On July 17, 1858, Lincoln visited Atlanta,
Illinois, and heard Douglas harangue a crowd but declined to speak himself.
His host, Sylvester Strong, asked for a picture. Soon after Lincoln's return to
Springfield, he sent Strong this ambrotype, now in the Ostendorf collection.

24

A. L. Marsch collection O-13

His HAIR IS CUT AND COMBED in this photograph, cameraman and place unknown, about 1858. A Civil War soldier from Parma, Ohio, was the original
owner of this portrait, published in the *Cleveland Plain Dealer* on February 12,
1942, from a print in the Marsch collection. Possibly it is a photographic copy
of one of two daguerreotypes, both now lost, taken in Ohio in 1859.

HIS HAIR IS LONG AND MUSSED in this unique tintype (O–12) taken about 1858 by an unknown photographer and first published by Ida M. Tarbell from a copy owned by artist Truman H. Bartlett of Boston. This is the only extant *original* tintype of Lincoln, although a few paper photographs were later copied on tintypes for use as campaign badges.

Made of black japanned iron, the tintype (often called ferrotype or melaino-type) was produced by the collodion or wet-plate process. Like the daguerreo-type, it could not be used as a negative, but it was cheap and practically indestructible. Using a nine-tube camera, a photographer could take thirty-six pictures with four exposures and four moves of a large plate, afterwards cutting apart the separate pictures with tin snips.

Published here through the courtesy of the National Lincoln Museum (Old Ford's Theatre).

SIX CITIES CLAIM THIS PHOTOGRAPH, probably by Roderick M. Cole of Peoria,
about 1858.

Ostendorf collection
Tintype Variant (Reversed) O–14

WIDELY REPRODUCED on campaign ribbons of 1860, this portrait underscores the determination in the candidate's face. Lincoln liked it and often signed photographic prints for admirers. He gave a copy to his stepmother in 1861.

Fifty years of research have failed to fix beyond doubt the date or the place where it was taken. Some of the early prints bear contemporary inscriptions on its origin, but these assertions do not gibe. Ascribed to Monmouth, Springfield, Peoria, and Pittsfield in Illinois; Dayton, Ohio; and Hannibal, Missouri—this photograph has only one city to go before it equals Homer's record of being claimed by seven cities.

By far the strongest claim comes from Peoria, visited several times by Lincoln in 1858. Here Henry H. Cole opened an ambrotype and photographic gallery about 1857. In his old age, Cole claimed to have photographed Lincoln. But his brother, Roderick M. Cole, listed in the 1856 city directory as a daguerreotypist, was more likely the cameraman. On July 3, 1905, R. M. Cole wrote to Judge McCulloch, one of the founders of the Illinois State Historical Library: ". . . the Photo you have of Abraham Lincoln is a copy of a Dagueratype [*sic*], that I made in my gallery in this city [Peoria] during the Lincoln and Douglas campaign.

"I invited him to my gallery to give me a sitting . . . and when I had my plate ready, he said to me, 'I cannot see why all you artists want a likeness of me unless it is because I am the homeliest man in the State of Illinois.' "

Meserve collection   Variant O–14

29

Lincoln National Life Foundation   O–16

PHOTOGRAPH BY Samuel M. Fassett, Chicago, Illinois, October 4, 1859. Lincoln posed for this portrait at the gallery of Cooke and Fassett in Chicago, and Cooke, who had asked Lincoln for the sitting, wrote on April 25, 1865, to his partner: "Mrs. Lincoln pronounced [it] the best likeness she had ever seen of her husband." The negative of this rare photograph was destroyed in the Chicago fire.

Chicago Historical Society   Variant O–16

Ostendorf collection O–15

A PHOTOGRAPH OF UNKNOWN ORIGIN by an unidentified cameraman, probably taken about 1859 in Springfield, Illinois. J. C. Browne of Philadelphia thought it was taken in 1858; H. W. Fay claimed it was the work of Frederick Gutekunst of Philadelphia; others assert that it was taken by William Seavy in Springfield at the same sitting as a similar pose (O–30), but this is impossible, for Lincoln's clothes are different. A brief pen portrait of Lincoln by Moncure D. Conway, September 17, 1859, fits this likeness: "The face had a battered and bronzed look . . . and an expression of sadness."

31

LINCOLN KNEW AND LIKED THESE ANIMALS. The stories about Lincoln's affection for animals are many—how he climbed a tree to put a small bird back into its nest, pulled a squealing pig from the mud, or plunged into freezing water to rescue his dog from an ice floe. Pictured here are two animals he knew intimately and which shared his life.

Lincoln allowed his boys, Willie and Tad, to have all the pets they wished, and the result was a family menagerie of cats, turtles, white rats, frogs, chicks, dogs, and a talking crow.

PRESIDENT LINCOLN'S HORSE. "OLD ROBIN."

Ostendorf collection

OLD ROBIN IN FRONT OF THE SPRINGFIELD HOME. Photograph of Lincoln's horse by F. W. Ingmire of Springfield. The two men with "Old Bob," as he was nicknamed, are Rev. Brown (left) and Rev. Trevan. Other horses owned by Lincoln were "Old Tom," his first circuit horse, and "Old Buck," about 1850–55.

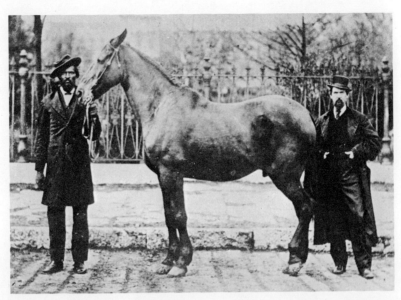

Ostendorf collection

OLD ROBIN SURVIVED HIS FAMOUS MASTER. Another photograph of Lincoln's horse taken in Springfield on the day of the President's funeral. The man is John Flynn, who purchased the horse from Lincoln on January 23, 1861. With Flynn is a Negro groom.

THREE PHOTOGRAPHS OF FIDO by F. W. Ingmire of Springfield, taken early in 1861. When Lincoln and his family left for Washington, this family pet was presented to John and Frank Roll, playmates of Willie and Tad.

Illinois State Historical Society

Ostendorf collection O-17

THE PHOTOGRAPH THAT MADE LINCOLN PRESIDENT

"They got my shadow," Lincoln wrote, "and can multiply copies indefinitely."

ON THE LEFT is the most famous of the beardless poses, taken by Mathew B. Brady on Monday morning, February 27, 1860, only a few hours before Lincoln delivered his Cooper Union address. That speech and this portrait, Lincoln afterwards said, put him in the White House.

Two days before the sitting Lincoln had arrived in New York, his clothes wrinkled, his address not fully prepared. Henry C. Bowen, editor of the *Independent*, who had promoted the speech but did not know the orator personally, met him and was jolted by the apparition. Carrying only "an old-fashioned comical-looking carpet-bag," the tall stranger was "travel-stained and looked tired and woe-begone." The following Monday when Brady put his camera eye on him, Lincoln was more refreshed, but his costume had not improved. His neck stuck out of his collar like a turtle's, and Brady had trouble shortening it.

The result shows that Brady not only knew how to take a photograph but how to retouch it. For although he caught Lincoln's left eye roving upward, he skillfully took out the harsh lines in the campaigner's face and yet kept all the intensity of his expression.

One of those who met with Lincoln on his arrival in New York was journalist Richard Cunningham McCormick. "We visited a photographic establishment [Brady's] upon the corner of Broadway and Bleecker streets," wrote McCormick in 1865, "where he sat for his picture, the first taken in New York. . . . From the gallery we returned to the Astor House, and found that the arrangements for his appearance at the Cooper Institute on the same evening (February 27th) had been completed."

THE CARTE-DE-VISITE PHOTOGRAPH, introduced in 1859, helped to make the Brady Cooper Union portrait known to almost every American.

Named after the French visiting card, the carte photograph was a paper print from a wet-plate or collodion glass negative, mounted on a card about 2¼ by 4 inches. Cartes-de-visite were popular from 1860 to 1866 and were eagerly collected in albums. At one time the Anthony firm was daily turning out 3,600 such photographs of celebrities, including many of Lincoln.

The Brady Cooper Union portrait was also line-engraved in newspapers and books, lithographed for drawing rooms, and copied on campaign posters and buttons.

U.I. Harris collection
Variant O–17

REVERSED TINTYPE
1860 CAMPAIGN BUTTON

ENGRAVED CARTE-DE-VISITE PORTRAIT

Ostendorf collection   Variant O–17

REPUBLICAN CANDIDATE, 1860
With his features completely
altered by retouching,
Lincoln looks like a
birdwatcher.

Smithsonian Institution (M-124) O-24

MEDAL FROM RETOUCHED PHOTOGRAPH
Dies were engraved by George H. Lovett
and cut by Henning and Eymann,
New York, 1860.

Lincoln National Life Foundation

Ostendorf collection Restored O–24

THE ORIGINAL PHOTOGRAPH RESTORED

HIS FEATURES "PRETTIED" with India ink, Lincoln is almost unrecognizable. The lines in his face are painted out; the chin is built up; the aquiline nose is remodeled; the cheekbone is lowered; the hair is artistically combed; the eyelids are lifted; and even the famous mole is subdued. The original photograph, possibly taken at Springfield in May, 1860, is nearly obliterated by the artist's ink "improvements."

This profile portrait (O–24) was probably taken by William Marsh of Springfield at the written request of Colonel William L. Bramhall, who had met Lincoln three months earlier at a special dinner on the day of the Cooper Union speech, February 27, 1860. "The photograph came even sooner than I expected," recorded Bramhall. "I determined to have struck at my own expense a campaign medal bearing the likeness of the party choice."

The removal of the heavy India-ink lines and the strengthening of the original sepia tones has restored the portrait almost to its original appearance.

39

THE "BIGGEST MAN" AT THE DECATUR CONVENTION photographed by Edward A. Barnwell, Decatur, May 9, 1860. Barnwell wanted a portrait of the "biggest [tallest] man" at the Decatur Republican Convention, who, he was told, was a likely nominee. He hunted up Lincoln and was granted a sitting. On May 10, the following day, the delegates endorsed Lincoln.

Lost for many years, this unusual portrait (O–19) was presented by the photographer's daughter, Grace, to the Decatur Public Library in 1947.

For the first time the cord to Lincoln's spectacles is clearly visible in a photograph.

41

Lincoln National Life Foundation

LINCOLN LIFTS HIS EYES UPWARD in this photograph (O–20) by William Marsh, Springfield, Illinois, May 20, 1860. Visited by Republican Convention delegate Marcus L. Ward of Newark, New Jersey, two days after his nomination, Lincoln was asked for a photograph. "He replied," wrote Ward, "that he had not a satisfactory one, 'but then,' he added, 'we will walk out together and I will sit for one.'"

Long attributed to "William Church," this portrait was actually taken by William Marsh, listed in the 1860–61 Springfield City Directory as "Photographer, Ambrotypes, W.S. Public Square." No William Church appeared in the directory.

Ostendorf collection
Variant O–21

Chicago Historical Society   O–21

HE LOOKS STRAIGHT INTO THE CAMERA. A second pose at the same sitting by William Marsh, Springfield, Illinois, May 20, 1860. Between exposures Lincoln used his fingers to comb what Sir William Howard Russell called his "thatch of wild Republican hair." In both pictures Lincoln's spectacles cord is visible across his white shirt.

The previous attribution of this and its companion pose to an imaginary William Church was perhaps caused by the misreading of an early identification. When written in the florid script of the last century, a capital "M" closely resembles "Ch," and after this alteration, it would be easy to read a "u" for an "a" and a "c" for an "s" to turn the name "Marsh" into "Church."

43

SIX DAYS AFTER HIS NOMINATION, this ambrotype, probably by William Marsh, Springfield, May 24, 1860, was taken at the suggestion of Lincoln's campaign biographer, Joseph H. Barrett, who needed a photograph as the frontispiece for his *Life of Abraham Lincoln* (Cincinnati, 1860). Wrote Barrett: "At my request and in my presence (May 24, 1860) he sat for a daguerreotype [a term used for ambrotypes mounted in daguerreotype cases] which was lithographically reproduced for the volume then in preparation, published the following month."

Previous biographers have assigned this photograph to the sitting of May 20, but notice that Lincoln's spectacles cord is not visible and his tie is knotted differently.

Ostendorf collection   O–23

A RETOUCHED POSE AT THE SAME SITTING. Ambrotype, probably by William Marsh, Springfield, May 24, 1860. This recently discovered photographic copy of an ambrotype was obviously taken at the same time as the portrait opposite. The tie is identical and no spectacles cord is shown; but an artist has painted in a background and retouched the features. A colored variation with a beard added was engraved by E. B. and E. C. Kellogg of Hartford, Connecticut, and published in 1861 by George Whiting of New York.

"THE PECULIAR CURVE OF THE LOWER LIP" is visible in this photograph by Alexander Hesler of Chicago, taken at Springfield, Illinois, June 3, 1860. On this same day Hesler, who also took the second known photograph of Lincoln (O-2), made three other portraits of the Republican nominee. Wrote Lincoln's law partner, William H. Herndon: "There is the peculiar curve of the lower lip, the lone mole on the right cheek, and a pose of the head so essentially Lincolnian; no other artist has ever caught it."

Chicago Historical Society   O–27

A PHOTOGRAPH WHICH PLEASED LINCOLN, taken by Alexander Hesler, Springfield, Illinois, June 3, 1860. Of this and the portrait opposite, Lincoln said,
"That looks better and expresses me better than any I have ever seen; if it
pleases the people I am satisfied."

47

Meserve collection O–28

"My homely face"—Abraham Lincoln

Photograph by Alexander Hesler, Springfield, Illinois, June 3, 1860. Not long after Lincoln's nomination, a Chicago reporter visited his home and noticed a framed photograph over the sofa. Likely it was one of the Hesler poses, perhaps the one at left. Observed the nominee: "That picture gives a very fair representation of my homely face."

Illinois State Historical Library   Variant O–28

Small variant shows full view.

A SIMILAR POSE with the hard lines removed. Despite the prettying, Lincoln's features are strong and his remarkable nose, as Sir William Howard Russell noted, "stands out from the face, with an inquiring, anxious air, as though it was sniffing for some good thing in the wind."

Ostendorf collection O–29

THE LAST OF THE FOUR PORTRAITS by Alexander Hesler, Springfield, Illinois, June 3, 1860. Criticized by Republican leaders for the famous "tousled hair" photograph (O–2), Hesler was asked to take some campaign pictures which would show a more handsome candidate. Lincoln was unable to go to Hesler's studio in Chicago, but he agreed to get "dressed up" for the sitting if the photographer would come to Springfield. Hesler came, and set up his camera near a large window in the old Capitol Building. It was a quiet Sunday and Hesler worked undisturbed with Lincoln. He took these four splendid poses, two of which (O–26 and O–27) sold about 10,000 copies!

The original plates were retained by George B. Ayres when he bought and sold the Hesler gallery right after the Civil War. In 1881, Ayres made some fine prints direct from the plates, at the same time producing a duplicate set of glass negatives. In 1933 the original plates were cracked in the mail. The post office paid the claim and presented the broken negatives to the Smithsonian Institution. The duplicate plates are now owned by the Chicago Historical Society.

BRIGHT LIGHTING SOFTENS HIS FEATURES. This photograph by an unknown cameraman was posed in Chicago a few days before Lincoln returned to Springfield on April 5, 1860. The negative was sent to M. C. Tuttle in St. Paul for use in printing campaign portraits. It arrived broken. Lincoln presented the only surviving print to William C. Bane, from whom it passed to Bane's neighbor, the present owner, Gilbert L. Ross of Lake Geneva, Wisconsin.

Lincoln's features seem youthful and almost happy. William H. Herndon, the law partner who knew him in all his moods, noted that there were times when "it appeared as if Lincoln's soul was fresh from its creator."

Lincoln National Life Foundation   O–32

SUBDUED LIGHT MAKES HIS FACE RUGGED in this photograph by an unknown artist, Springfield, about June, 1860. The sharp cleavage of light and shadow gives strength to the candidate's features. This portrait suggests the description of Lincoln by a London journalist: "An honest old lawyer, with a face half Roman, half Indian, wasted by climate, scarred by a life's struggle."

After the glass negative of the preceding portrait (O–18) was accidentally broken, Lincoln showed a Springfield photographer his only print and asked for a picture "something about like that." The result is this almost identical pose. The negative was sent to M. C. Tuttle of St. Paul and prints were widely distributed during the Presidential campaign.

51

PHOTOGRAPH BY AN UNKNOWN ARTIST in Springfield, apparently made about the same time as the preceding portrait (O–32), for the hair, suit, tie, and collar are similar. The background was painted out, but the face is unretouched. An old and improbable legend has it that Alexander Hesler discarded this picture and his successor dug it out of the studio wastebasket.

A correspondent from the New York *Herald* visited Lincoln in 1860 and wrote: "There is no appearance of age about the man. How they call him 'Old Abe' I do not see. You can hardly detect the presence of frost on his black hair."

Ostendorf collection O-30

A PHOTOGRAPH FROM AN OLD SCRAPBOOK, by William Seavy, Springfield, taken in the summer of 1860. Pasted in an early campaign scrapbook, this portrait bears a notation by the original owner, N. S. Wright: "Taken by William Seavy, 1860." Although Seavy's gallery was located in Canton, Illinois, he traveled to Springfield to photograph the candidate. After this single print was made, the negative was lost when fire destroyed his gallery.

Courtesy Allegheny College   O-35

LONG-HIDDEN profile photograph by an unknown cameraman, Springfield, summer of 1860.

Although Lincoln expert Ida M. Tarbell published many Lincoln photographs, she never released her print of this beardless profile. It was found among the papers she willed to Allegheny College. Another print turned up in the effects of the artist, John Henry Brown. Since it is not one of the ambrotypes taken at the special sitting for Brown on August 13, 1860 (the candidate is here wearing a different vest), it is possible that Lincoln himself gave it to Brown as an aid in his study of Lincoln's features.

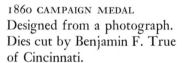
1860 CAMPAIGN MEDAL
Designed from a photograph. Dies cut by Benjamin F. True of Cincinnati.

Meserve collection O–25

BECAUSE IT WAS DISCARDED IN A WOODSHED, this faded photograph by Joseph Hill, Springfield, June, 1860, escaped a blaze which destroyed all the photographs and negatives in Hill's gallery. The photographer lived to be ninety, and on September 25, 1913, he reminisced of Lincoln: "I shall never forget how he looked. He had on white trousers, a sort of figured silk vest and a long, black coat."

Ostendorf collection O-38

WITH HIS SON WILLIE, Lincoln stands on the terrace of the only house he ever owned. He called it his "little brown cottage" and bought it for $1,500 in 1844 from the Reverend Charles Dresser, an Episcopal rector who had married the Lincolns in 1842. Here Lincoln's sons, Eddie, Willie, and Tad, were born, and here he was living when elected President.

This picture of Lincoln at home was taken in the summer of 1860 by John Adams Whipple of Boston, who had set up his camera in the yard across the street.

56

tendorf collection   Detail O–38

IMPISH TAD peeks out from behind the corner post in this detail enlargement of the preceding picture. His face is slightly blurred because he did not hold his pose for the full camera exposure count, but his father and Willie both gripped the poles to maintain a rigid stance. The children in the foreground (one of whom is shown here) are unidentified.

Just a few months before this picture was taken, Major George Haven Putnam of New York met Lincoln and got an unfavorable impression of "the long, ungainly figure, upon which hung clothes that . . . were evidently the work of an unskillful tailor; the clumsy hands . . . the long, gaunt head capped by a shock of hair that seemed not to have been thoroughly brushed."

THE LINCOLN BOYS, William Wallace ("Willie"), ten (left below), and his brother Thomas ("Tad"), seven, pose earnestly for a Springfield photographer in 1860. Willie was bright and serious; Tad was roguish and spoiled. The oldest son, Robert Todd, seventeen, was attending Exeter Academy in New Hampshire. The second son, Edward Baker, had died at the age of four in 1850.

WILLIE AND TAD appear informally in this detail enlargement (right) of the photograph on the next page. Tad leans on the post for support during the camera exposure, while his father and Willie continue to steady themselves on the pales.

Ostendorf collection O—

Ostendorf collection

Ostendorf collection

58

Ostendorf collection O-39

A MAN WHO OUTLIVED LINCOLN by seventy-eight years, Isaac Diller, playmate of the Lincoln boys, appears in this second photograph by John Adams Whipple of Boston, taken at the same time in the summer of 1860. Diller survived every person who was photographed with Lincoln. He stands on the sidewalk, almost directly under the corner pillar of the paling. Shortly before his death at eighty-nine in 1943, he explained why his figure is so indistinct: "I ran across the street from my aunt's house to get in a free picture with the Lincolns, but I turned my head at the wrong moment to look at a farm wagon. Only the stripes on my socks and my boots showed up."

59

Chicago Historical Society O–34

A JOYOUS CROWD CHEERS ITS CANDIDATE in this photograph by an unknown cameraman, Springfield, August 8, 1860. After a huge Republican rally in the morning, enthusiastic Lincoln supporters, many of them close friends and neighbors of the nominee, gathered at midday in front of his home. They carried banners bearing the slogan "Won't you let me in, Kansas."

Diller was there and later wrote: "I witnessed this parade from a point opposite the Lincoln home, August 8, 1860, and all day wore a blue ribbon with a picture of Abraham Lincoln pasted on it."

HE POSES BUT DECLINES TO SPEAK. In this enlargement of the photograph on the left, Lincoln appears tall and gaunt in his white suit. His rumpled hair, with a lock tumbling over his forehead, gives him a casual air. The journalist Donn Piatt met Lincoln shortly before he was elected President. "Tall as he was," recorded Piatt, "his hands and feet looked out of proportion, so long and clumsy were they. Every movement was awkward in the extreme. He sat with one leg thrown over the other, and the pendant foot swung almost to the floor. And all the while, two little boys, his sons, clambered over those legs, patted his cheeks, pulled his nose, and poked their fingers in his eyes, without causing reprimand or even notice. He had a face that defied artistic skill to soften or idealize. . . . It was capable of few expressions, but those were extremely striking. When in repose, his face was dull, heavy, and repellent. It brightened, like a lit lantern, when animated."

Ostendorf collection   Detail O-34

"HARD LINES IN HIS FACE" show in this ambrotype by Preston Butler, Springfield, Monday, August 13, 1860. This pose and the similar one opposite were made for the portrait painter, John Henry Brown, noted for his miniatures on ivory. Brown arrived in Springfield on August 12 with a commission from Judge John M. Read of Philadelphia to paint a good-looking miniature of Lincoln "whether or not the subject justified it"! Brown went with Lincoln to Butler's daguerreotype studio, where Butler took six ambrotypes, of which only these two survive.

"There are so many hard lines in his face," wrote Brown in his diary, "that it becomes a mask to the inner man. His true character only shines out when in an animated conversation, or when telling an amusing tale. . . . He is said to be a homely man; I do not think so."

Ostendorf collection O-37

Meserve collection   O–36

 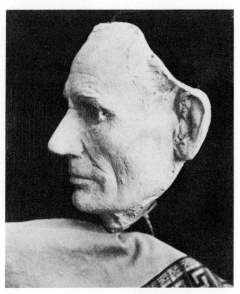

Meserve collection   Ostendorf collection

"THERE IS THE ANIMAL HIMSELF"—Lincoln to Volk, on seeing this plaster mask.

This portrait in plaster made by Leonard Wells Volk, Chicago, Saturday, March 31, 1860, has an immediacy which admirably supplements the photographs of Lincoln.

Leonard W. Volk made the mask between court sessions while Lincoln was in Chicago as counsel in the famous Sand Bar case, a dispute over lands north of the Chicago River. The sculptor put quills in Lincoln's nose to permit breathing, then applied wet plaster to his face, an operation which took about an hour. After the plaster had set, Lincoln gradually worked the mask off, pulling a few hairs from his temple. It hurt, and his eyes watered. Later he commented that "the process was anything but agreeable."

Chicago Historical Society

VOLK AT WORK ON HIS LINCOLN BUST. The life mask of Lincoln was made by Volk as a model for the plaster bust shown here on his work bench. The sculptor had just completed a bust of his wife's cousin, Stephen A. Douglas. This bust also appears in the photograph.

Ostendorf collection   O–37

THE LAST BEARDLESS PORTRAIT, an ambrotype by Preston Butler, taken at his daguerreotype studio in Springfield, August 13, 1860, was made at the request of the miniaturist, John Henry Brown of Philadelphia. Lincoln's lips are firmly set, but there is a half-twinkle in his eyes. Earlier in the summer the journalist Charles C. Coffin had called upon the candidate and noted "a sincerity which won instant confidence. The lines upon his face, the large ears, sunken cheeks, enormous nose, shaggy hair, the deep-set eyes, sparkling with humor, and which seemed to be looking far away, were distinguishing facial marks . . . a stranger meeting him on a country road, ignorant of his history, would have said, 'He is no ordinary man'."

66

Herbert Wells Fay collection O–40

Left: THE FIRST WHISKERS SPROUT. Photograph by Samuel G. Alschuler, Chicago, Sunday, November 25, 1860. Picturing the President-elect with a half-beard, this unique portrait was preserved by Henry C. Whitney, a youthful attorney who had traveled the Illinois circuit with Lincoln. Some thirty years later it turned up in the files of Chicago photographer C. D. Mosher, and was saved from destruction by Herbert Wells Fay, a custodian of the Lincoln tomb.

"BILLY, let's give them a chance to grow," said Lincoln to his barber, William Florville, who was sharpening his razor to shave off the newly sprouted whiskers.

A little girl named Grace Bedell had urged Lincoln to "let your whiskers grow," to which the President-elect had answered, "Do you not think people would call it a piece of silly affection?" Probably he decided on a beard partly as a concession to the new fashion and partly to save himself the trouble of shaving each morning. Quipped a newsman, "Old Abe is . . . puttin' on (h)airs."

Right: RESULT: A NEAT BEARD. Unretouched photograph by C. S. German, Springfield, probably taken on Sunday, January 13, 1861. This first portrait of Lincoln with a full beard was made at the request of Ohio sculptor Thomas D. Jones, who had come to Springfield to make a bust of Lincoln from life.

Meserve collection O–41

LINCOLN'S FIRST PHOTOGRAPH WITH A FULL BEARD, by C. S. German at his National Gallery on the West Side of the Public Square, Springfield, Illinois, about Sunday, January 13, 1861. It is more of a profile than the opposite companion pose. On Sunday, presumably January 13 or January 20, 1861, sculptor Thomas D. Jones accompanied Lincoln to a photographic gallery "to pose him for some pictures he desired to present to a very dear friend."

Lincoln National Life Foundation O-42

RARE, UNPUBLISHED PORTRAIT.   Although very similar to the preceding pose and made at the same sitting, this handsome photograph is more of a full face. Notice that a larger part of Lincoln's cheek and less of the hair at the back of his head is visible. The difference between these two photographs is much greater than in a stereographic pair (made simultaneously with two adjoining camera lenses). Yet because this portrait so closely resembles the companion pose, it escaped notice until recently when it was discovered by Lloyd Ostendorf in the Lincoln National Life Foundation.

Lincoln National Life Foundation   O-43

THE LAST SITTING IN SPRINGFIELD, a photograph by C. S. German, Springfield, February 9, 1861, two days before Lincoln left for Washington. The heavy beard softens the lines in his face, and makes him less gaunt. His eyes are lifted, giving the features a benign, almost saintly expression. He is now the man whom tens of thousands of Union soldiers will shortly know as "Father Abraham."

70

Meserve collection O–44

PUBLISHED

THE FIRST BEARDED PROFILES. *Left:* Photograph by C. S. German, Springfield, February 9, 1861, taken during the same sitting as the photograph on the preceding page. *Below right:* A second profile, and the third photograph, made by C. S. German on February 9, 1861. Recently discovered and published here for the first time, this interesting profile reveals more of the back of Lincoln's head than any other portrait. Notice that the President-elect has shifted his body, and his left coat lapel, clearly shown in the first profile, is no longer visible.

When the new President came to Washington, it was fashionable to ridicule his awkward manners and homeliness. Many were astonished to discover he was almost handsome. "I was struck with the simplicity, kindness, and dignity of his deportment," wrote *New York Times* reporter John M. Winchell, "so different from the clownish manners with which it was then customary to invest him. His face was a pleasant surprise, formed as my expectations had been from the poor photographs then in vogue, and the general belief in his ugliness. I remember thinking how much better-looking he was than I had anticipated, and wondering that any one should consider him ugly."

Ostendorf collection O–45

UNPUBLISHED

ON THE WAY TO WASHINGTON he raises the flag at Independence Hall. One of three photographs by F. DeBourg Richards, Philadelphia, Pennsylvania, Friday, February 22, 1861, shortly after sunrise.

THE FIRST PHOTOGRAPHS OF A PRESIDENT-ELECT. Soldiers at attention and men and boys perched in the trees watch the President-elect hoist the stars and stripes at Independence Hall. Lincoln stands, hat off, directly above the single star on the extreme left of the draped flag. His son Tad, hat on, rests his arm on the rail above the cluster of stars on the right.

The flag-raising is in honor of the admission of Kansas to the Union. A reporter related that Lincoln's "appearance was greeted with applause and cheering by the tremendous crowd." Stephen Benton introduced the President-elect and invited him "personally to raise this new American flag." Lincoln rolled up his sleeves for the task. Warnings of a plot against his life did not deter him from making a plea for the American principle of equality. "I would rather be assassinated on this spot," he declared, "than surrender it."

To elude possible assassins, Lincoln finished his journey to Washington in secret on a special train, accompanied only by his close friend and bodyguard, Ward Hill Lamon, who carried "a brace of fine pistols, a huge bowie-knife, a blackjack, a pair of brass knuckles, and a hickory cudgel."

Meserve collection O–48

LINCOLN IS CLOSER to the center of the flag, standing bare-headed above the third star from the left. Photograph by F. DeB. Richards, Philadelphia, Pennsylvania, February 22, 1861, shortly after sunrise. Tad leans on the rail with chin in hand, gazing at the spectators.

Historical Society of Pennsylvania   O–46

ANOTHER VIEW OF THE FLAG-RAISING. Photograph by F. DeB. Richards,
Philadelphia, Pennsylvania, Friday, February 22, 1861, shortly after dawn.
The closed windows of the Hall and the absence of the troops and of the boys
in the trees indicate that this picture was probably the earliest of this series. One
old print bears a contemporary notation on the back: "Lincoln at flag raising,
Philadelphia."

ːI A   O–51B   O–51C

THE FIRST SITTING IN WASHINGTON. Taken with a three-lens camera on a single glass plate, long ago cut apart, the three images are here assembled for the first time from old photographs in the Ostendorf collection. The photograph on the preceding page is an enlargement of the center image.

EXHAUSTED BY A TRAIN JOURNEY during which he had traveled nearly two thousand miles and visited seven states, Lincoln went to Brady's Washington studio, probably on Sunday, February 24, 1861, and sat (opposite), absorbed in problems, while Alexander Gardner took five poses.

Youthful artist George H. Story, friend and associate of Brady, was at the sitting, and fifty-five years later recalled: "It was in November of the year 1859 that I went to Washington, D. C. and set up my easel in a room . . . which I hired from M. B. Brady. . . . A day or two after the President's arrival [February 23, 1861] Mr. Gardner, Mr. Brady's representative in Washington, came to my room and asked me to come and pose Mr. Lincoln for a picture. When I entered the room the President was seated in a chair wholly absorbed in deep thought. . . . I said in an undertone to the operator, 'bring your instrument here and take the picture.'"

O-49B

O–49A   O–49B   O–49C

REASSEMBLED three-lens collodion plate (Ostendorf collection), from which the center image was enlarged for the preceding page.

APPARENTLY CONCERNED about the time the photographer was taking to prepare the lighting and plates, the harried President-elect has just looked at the watch which he holds, case still open, in his right hand.

The three-lens camera used by Gardner was devised to produce three almost identical negatives on a single large glass (or collodion) plate, about 4½ by 8 inches. The three negatives on one plate made possible a much faster reproduction of photographs.

At this first Washington sitting, Gardner also used a two-lens, or stereoscopic, camera.

Meserve collection O-50B

LINCOLN'S RIGHT HAND IS BADLY SWOLLEN in this photograph by Alexander Gardner, Brady's Gallery, Pennsylvania Avenue, Washington, D. C., probably Sunday, February 24, 1861. During his journey to Washington, Lincoln shook thousands of hands. Throughout the sitting he kept his swollen right hand closed or out of sight.

Meserve collection (M-118) O-50A   Meserve collection (M-168) O-50B

REASSEMBLED STEREOGRAPH PLATE

"THE STEREOSCOPE IS A LEAF torn from the book of God's recording angel!" exclaimed poet Oliver Wendell Holmes. The stereo or three-dimension camera had two lenses set several inches apart on a horizontal plane, approximately the position of human eyes. These lenses, taking simultaneous photographs, recorded perfectly the two images which, when seen by human eyes, are fused in the brain to create perspective. Although the two pictures thus taken appear to be identical, they actually vary slightly in position.

EARLY STEREOSCOPIC CAMERA
used by Mathew B. Brady (1861–70)

Courtesy Graflex collection and
George Eastman House, Rochester, N. Y.

O-53A

HE SEEMS LOST IN A REVERIE. Multiple-lens photograph by Alexander Gardner, Brady's Gallery, Pennsylvania Avenue, Washington, D. C., probably Sunday, February 24, 1861.

Any two of these photographs viewed through a stereoscope would reveal a third dimension, but a more perfect stereo quality may be obtained by combining the first and third images.

During the Civil War the stereoscope was very popular and was often found, with a basket of stereo views, on the parlor table. It is astonishing that Lincoln was not more often photographed by the stereo camera, for Brady and other cameramen frequently used stereoscopic equipment to record military and civil scenes.

By the use of three- and four-lens cameras, the photographer of the Civil War unintentionally produced pictures which, when properly mounted in pairs and viewed through a stereoscope, create the illusion of a third dimension.

Ostendorf collection O-53 A   Ostendorf collection O-53 B   Ostendorf collection O-53 C

REASSEMBLED THREE-LENS PLATE

"THAT SERIOUS FAR-AWAY LOOK"—*John G. Nicolay*. Multiple-lens photograph by Alexander Gardner, Brady's Gallery, Pennsylvania Avenue, Washington, D. C., probably Sunday, February 24, 1861.

An engraved reproduction of this photograph was published in *Harper's Weekly* for April 27, 1861.

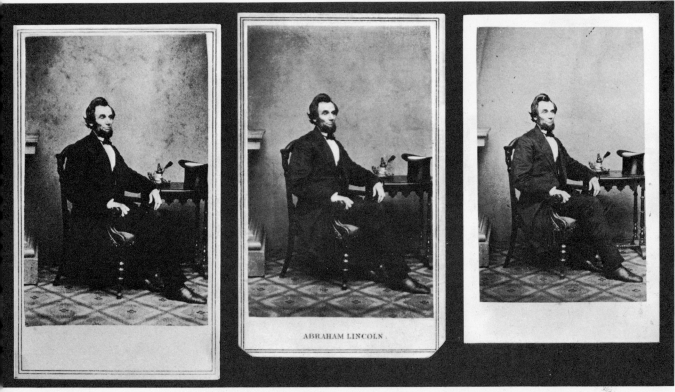

Ostendorf collection O–52 A   Ostendorf collection O–52 B   Ostendorf collection O–52 C

LINCOLN'S BEARD EXCITED MUCH INTEREST during his trip to Washington. About two days before his first sitting at the gallery, the *North American and United States Gazette* of Philadelphia commented: "We never before placed the proper estimate upon the picturesqueness of whiskers. Mr. Lincoln with whiskers is anything but the reverse of good-looking. His beard should never again be laid aside; with it he is a fine looking personage."

The first sitting in Washington was held for *Harper's Weekly*, apparently to satisfy public curiosity about Lincoln's beard. The President-elect posed in his best attire. George H. Story recalled that he seemed "elegant in dress and appearance, his clothes being made of the finest broadcloth."

During the sitting the exhausted President-elect scarcely moved. The wrinkles in his coat and in the sleeve of his tired right arm remained virtually unchanged throughout the five poses.

In printing an engraving of the photograph opposite (O–52 B), *Harper's Weekly* noted: "We publish herewith, from a photograph just taken expressly for this paper, a PORTRAIT OF THE PRESIDENT . . . ."

Ostendorf collection O-

THE FIRST INAUGURAL.   A distant photograph from a special platform, by an unknown photographer, in front of the Capitol, Washington, D. C., afternoon of March 4, 1861.

"A small camera was directly in front of Mr. Lincoln," reported a newspaper, "another at a distance of a hundred yards, and a third of huge dimensions on the right, raised on a platform built specially for the purpose."

86

ENGRAVING FROM *Leslie's Illustrated Weekly*.
The new President wore steel-rimmed spectacles.

ENLARGEMENT OF INAUGURAL SCENE.
In this detail from the picture opposite
(O–54), Lincoln's face is obscured by shadows,
but his brand-new suit with its white shirt-front
and V-shaped frock coat is visible.

THE PRESIDENT-ELECT WAS DRESSED IN BLACK, with a black tie and a black silk
hat. He carried a cane. As he stepped forward to read his inaugural address, he
drew the manuscript from his breast pocket, placed it on the speaker's table,
and anchored it with his cane. Then he put on his spectacles and removed his
hat. Without hesitation, his former opponent, Stephen A. Douglas, reached
across the arm of reporter Henry Watterson and took the hat, keeping it on his
lap throughout the ceremonies. In a high-pitched but resonant voice, Lincoln
spoke for about half an hour, making a dramatic appeal for Southern loyalty.

The three photographers present had plenty of time to take pictures, yet
only the distant views have survived. The tall figure of Lincoln is partly hid-
den by the shadow of the wooden canopy.

For Mrs Lucy G. Speed, from whose pious hand I accepted the present of an Oxford Bible twenty years ago. Washington, D.C. October 3, 1861. A Lincoln.

J. B. Speed Art Museum, Louisville, Kentucky,
reproduced from an early unfaded copy. Ostendorf collection   O-55

PHOTOGRAPH, possibly by C. D. Fredricks of New York or James E. McClees or W. L. Germon of Philadelphia, probably taken between March 1, 1861, and June 30, 1861.

Ostendorf collection
Variant O-93

VARIANT BY
W. L. GERMON

A MYSTERY PORTRAIT of uncertain date and ascribed to several cameramen, including Brady, is this pose of the new President. Lincoln's round-tipped collar is different from that in any other picture. The length and intimacy of the inscription are unique also, for Lincoln seldom wrote more than a word or two on a photograph. Presented to the mother of Joshua F. Speed, most intimate of Lincoln's early friends, the original oval photograph, about 9 by 12 inches, is preserved in a gold frame. It is badly faded and shows evidence of slight retouching, but the inscription is clear and bold.

The portrait was long thought to date from about September, 1861, near the time of Lincoln's inscription, but printed on the back of one carte-de-visite reproduction, on a souvenir ticket to an Independence Day celebration, is this: "1776–1861 / Exhibition of Fireworks at the City Hall / (cut of flag) / July 4 –Admit the bearer–July 4." Thus the sitting definitely took place before July, 1861. Since Lincoln's hair was unusually long at his Brady sitting of February 24, 1861 (see O-53), but was cut before the "Speed" pose, the sitting was *after* February 24.

The attribution to Brady is based upon a letter of James B. Speed, grandson of Mrs. Speed, claiming that Lincoln had a special sitting for this photograph. The earlier date now established indicates that he presented the portrait to Lucy Speed as an afterthought and rules out Brady as photographer.

There are copies of the photograph which bear the imprints of C. D. Fredricks & Co., 587 Broadway, New York; W. L. Germon, 914 Arch Street, Philadelphia; and James E. McClees, 910 Chestnut Street, Philadelphia. Any of these men might have taken the photograph, but the recent discovery of a lithographic reproduction with the imprint "W. L. Germon Photo" indicates that Germon may have gone to Washington to take the picture.

Lincoln Memorial University   Variant O-93

VARIANT WITH FANCY BORDER

Courtesy Albert Morton Turner,
Orono, Maine

◄ FIRST PUBLICATION OF A RARE PHOTOGRAPH lost for a century. Enlargement from a carte-de-viste photograph by Edward Bierstadt, posed in or near Washington, D. C., about September, 1861. Although scholars have often noted that no camera portrait was taken of Lincoln during his first six months in office, it seemed probable to Lloyd Ostendorf that at least one was made, for there was intense public interest in our first bearded President and some galleries were even selling earlier photos on which beards were painted. Ostendorf's long search for the "undiscovered" photograph led him to New York, where, on October 6, 1956, in an old print and book shop, he found and bought for eight dollars the first known photograph of Lincoln as President. It is a superb study of the new Chief Executive.

EDWARD BIERSTADT, of the New Bedford Photographic Gallery, who photographed Lincoln in September, 1861.

OTHER PHOTOGRAPH BY BIERSTADT. Stereograph of picket guards near ⌐vinsville, Virginia, taken in the fall of 1861. Bierstadt operated a mobile ⌐ery and photographed many soldiers and military scenes in and near Wash-⌐ton, D. C.

1320 Picket Guard at rest, near Lewinsville, Va.

⌐tesy Albert Morton Turner, Orono, Maine

EDWARD BIERSTADT AT ABOUT EIGHTY

EDWARD BIERSTADT — LINCOLN'S UN-KNOWN PHOTOGRAPHER. Aided by his brother Charles, Edward Bierstadt ran a photographic studio in New Bedford. They were assisted in "artistic effects" by still another brother, the famous Western painter, Albert Bierstadt. The outbreak of the Civil War inspired Edward, as it did Brady and Gardner and many others, to bundle up his photographic equipment and "follow the Union troops." As a base of operations, Bierstadt chose a tavern in Langley, Virginia, about seven miles from Washington, where he boarded and kept his camera and chemicals. He drove from camp to camp with a wagon carrying portable equipment. For a while his mobile unit was at the headquarters of the 43d New York Infantry; then he set up shop with the 18th Massachusetts Infantry. Eventually he photographed many forts and military installations, but his open-air "gallery" also catered to the soldiers who wanted a likeness for their sweethearts or friends at home.

We do not know how Edward Bierstadt happened to photograph Lincoln, but it is quite possible that an introduction was supplied by his famous brother, Albert, or more likely, by Congressman Thomas Dawes Eliot, a supporter of Lincoln and a friend of the Bierstadt family. Perhaps no introduction was necessary, for the new President was easily approachable and spent much time visiting the army camps in and near Washington. Possibly the photographer merely asked the tall commander-in-chief to "step up and be photographed."

In October, 1861, Edward Bierstadt was called back to New Bedford by a serious family illness. The photograph of Lincoln was probably overlooked or forgotten during this crisis. Edward never returned to Washington. Soon after the war, he and his brother Charles dissolved their partnership. Edward settled in New York and went into business with his cousin, the noted printer, Theodore De Vinne. He developed various types of photographic plates, including a process for three-color lithography.

National Archives O-57

HIS EYES FLASH IN THIS GIANT IMPERIAL PHOTOGRAPH by Brady, probably taken in 1862 when Lincoln made his second visit to Brady's Washington gallery. The original collodion plate, largest-known of Lincoln, measures 18½ inches by 20⅜ inches. Lincoln's froglike left eyelid, which sometimes imparted a look of cunning to his features, is clearly caught by the camera. No doubt this is the expression observed by Colonel Theodore Lyman: "He has the look of sense and wonderful shrewdness, while the heavy eyelids give him a mark almost of genius."

Meserve collection   O-58A   Ostendorf collection   O-58B

TWO CARTES-DE-VISITE TAKEN SIMULTANEOUSLY by Brady, Washington, about 1862. After Brady and his staff had taken the imperial photograph on the preceding page. Lincoln held his pose until they moved the large camera away and brought up a multi-lens instrument. The original plates for this stereoscopic pair and for the three other multi-lens poses made at this sitting are now lost.

Ostendorf collection   O-58B

IN THIS ENLARGEMENT of the carte-de-visite photograph (O-58B), the slight differences between it and the imperial photograph (O-57) become apparent. The exposures were made only seconds apart.

Businessman Thomas B. Bancroft of Philadelphia met the President in the summer of 1862, about the time this photograph was made. "His appearance," he wrote, "almost justified the gibes and jeers with which his enemies were accustomed to describe him—all but his eyes; here his soul looked forth . . . piercing and searching; not to be deceived, yet practicing no guile."

95

"THE LONG AND THE SHORT OF IT" was Lincoln's humorous description of the twelve-inch difference between his height and his wife's. The President was six feet, four inches in his stocking feet; Mary Todd Lincoln was five feet, four. There is no photograph of them together, but in these accurately scaled and matching portraits the contrast is obvious and amusing. This picture of the President was taken by Gardner in 1863 and that of the First Lady by Brady in 1861.

Ostendorf collection   O–59

THE PRESIDENT SEEMS TENSE AND EAGER and there is a flash in his eyes. His secretary, John Hay, observed these probing eyes in action when he saw Lincoln fix his stare upon a brassy, overdressed fraud: "He looked through the man to the buttons on the back of his coat."

This damaged print, probably taken by Brady in Washington in 1862, is from the original glass negative, now lost or destroyed.

97

A RARE STEREO PORTRAIT, taken with a multi-lens camera and assembled here for the first time. The A or left image fits perfectly with the B or right image (from a scarce, stained print), thus forming a stereo pair.

An eighteen-year-old girl in Springfield noticed this meditative pose many times in the future President. Years later she told her son, Philip W. Ayres: "Always his thoughtful face was bent forward, as if thinking out some deep problem."

Ostendorf collection   O-60 A   Ostendorf collection   O-60 B

98

Ostendorf collection   O-60 A

ONE OF THE MOST CANDID OF LINCOLN PHOTOGRAPHS, this enlargement shows the President in a reflective mood. Possibly while Brady was loading his camera, Lincoln sank into a reverie, and the alert photographer, eager for so intimate a pose, asked him to hold the position.

Right: VIGNETTE HEAD by Brady, Washington, about 1862. Familiar to Lincoln scholars as Meserve No. 62, it is the head and shoulders of O–61 B.

Below: THREE VERY SLIGHTLY DIFFERENT carte-de-visite photographs of the profile view taken with a multi-lens at the second Brady sitting in Washington.

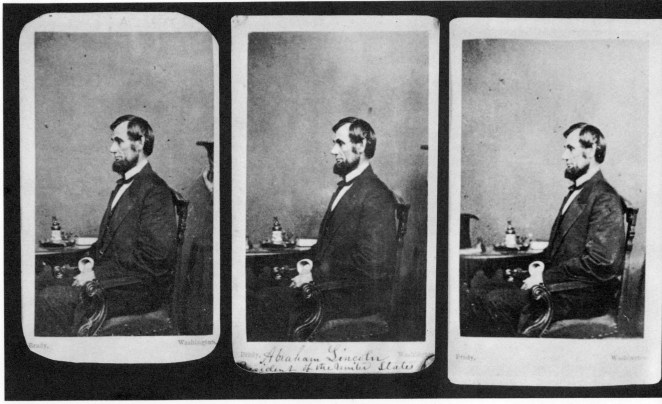

Ostendorf collection O–61 A   Meserve collection O–61 B   Meserve collection O–61 C

Brady, Washington.

Ostendorf collection O–61A

THE HABITUAL SADNESS which clung about Lincoln's features, often remarked upon by those who knew him, seems intensified in this enlarged profile view. "The melancholy seemed to roll from his shoulders and drip from the ends of his fingers," commented Governor Joseph W. Fifer of Illinois. Perhaps this Brady sitting took place in Washington soon after the death of Lincoln's son Willie, in February, 1862, an event which left the President so grief-stricken that he nearly lost his sanity.

Lincoln in motion pictures. This remarkable sequence of pictures, when projected as a movie on regular 35 mm. film, shows Lincoln in motion. The stereographs by Alexander Gardner (O–49 to O–53), all made at the same sitting, were skillfully edited and joined by the late Ken Snelling at Lloyd Ostendorf's suggestion to produce a series of frames in which the Civil War President, deep in thought, rouses from his meditation and turns his head to face the camera.

Lincoln, of course, never posed for a motion picture, since movies were not introduced until the 1890's. However, just a month before Lincoln's first inauguration, a device called the kinematoscope ("I see motion") was patented by Coleman Sellers. By the use of this mechanism a series of stereographs mounted on rotating blades gave the illusion of motion when watched through a viewer. The kinematoscope required a succession of meticulous poses for which the harried Chief Executive could scarcely be expected to sit. The best known of Sellers "movies" shows a man pounding a spike. How fascinating would be a kinematoscope of Lincoln splitting a rail or signing the Emancipation Proclamation!

First publication of a film copyrighted by Lloyd Ostendorf.

O-24   O-35

PROFILE OF GREATNESS—A comparison of all profile photographs.

Left: Two 1860 beardless profiles used as models for campaign medals. *Below:* The two bearded profiles at left were taken in Springfield in 1861; those at right were shot in 1862 at Washington, D. C., and at Antietam, Maryland.

Opposite page—*Above, at left and center:* The most famous profiles, 1864. *Above, right:* An 1863 profile. *Below, at left and center:* Profiles taken in the shade of McClellan's tent at Antietam, 1862. *Below, right:* Detail enlargement of outdoor photograph, taken in 1862.

O-44   O-45   O-61

O-89   O-80

THE CRAGGY PROFILE OF LINCOLN was often noted by his contemporaries. Wrote Judge Abram Bergen: "No complete idea of the irregularity of the profile of his features can be had from his pictures. . . . In the courtroom, while waiting for the Armstrong case to be called for trial, I . . . studied his face for two full hours. . . . His forehead protruded beyond his eyes more than two inches and retreated rapidly, about 25 degrees from the perpendicular. . . . From the front his eyes looked very deep-set and sunken, by reason of this abnormal extension of the frontal bone."

O-67   O-68

LINCOLN VISITS THE FRONT

DISTRESSED BECAUSE GENERAL MCCLELLAN HESITATED to attack Lee, the President goes to Antietam for a personal talk with the commander of the Army of the Potomac. He arrives late in the afternoon of October 2, 1862. In the picture (right), doubtless taken the next morning, he and "Little Mac" confront each other, surrounded by officers. Lincoln's thin, towering figure, accentuated by his plug hat, makes him the dominant personage in this group. Journalist Donn Piatt called him "a huge skeleton in clothes."

PHOTOGRAPH BY ALEXANDER GARDNER, operator for Mathew Brady, Antietam, Maryland, Tuesday, October 3, 1862.

Left to right: Colonel (later General) Delos B. Sacket; Major Montieth; General N. B. Sweitzer; General G. W. Morrell; General Andrew A. Humphreys; General George B. McClellan; Scout Adams; Colonel (later General) Alexander S. Webb; Captain (later General) George A. Custer; President Lincoln; General Lewis C. Hunt; General Fitz-John Porter; Allan Pinkerton; Colonel Fred T. Locke; Surgeon Letterman; Colonel R. N. Batchelder.

Library of Congress   O–63

HE BLINKS WHILE POSING WITH A DETECTIVE. Photograph from the original glass negative by Alexander Gardner, operator for Mathew Brady, Antietam, Maryland, Tuesday, October 3, 1862. On the left of the President stands Allan Pinkerton, noted detective and first chief of the Secret Service; on Lincoln's left is Major General John A. McClernand.

Library of Congress O-64

ANOTHER POSE WITH ALLAN PINKERTON. Photograph from the original glass negative by Alexander Gardner, operator for Mathew Brady, Antietam, Maryland, Tuesday, October 3, 1862. Lincoln again moves his head during the pose; and the detective, right hand thrust in his coat, continues his Napoleonic stance. A photographer's helper holds a newspaper on which an identification number is scratched.

THE PRESIDENT STANDS WHILE HIS BODYGUARD SITS. Stereo photograph by Alexander Gardner, operator for Mathew Brady, Antietam, Maryland, Tuesday, October 3, 1862.

Perhaps because Lincoln's friend and bodyguard, Ward Hill Lamon, was also wearing a plug hat and was nearly as tall as the President, the cameraman asked him to be seated so as not to draw attention from Lincoln, the central figure in the group. Lincoln dominates the soldiers around him precisely in the way that Governor John A. Andrew of Massachusetts remembered: "He stood, like Saul, among his veterans, head and shoulders above every man."

Ozias M. Hatch of Illinois identified the persons standing with the President, and this is believed to be the first publication with the identifications: *Left to right:* Buck Juit, a soldier; Lamon; Ozias M. Hatch; Marcy; Reeves; General McClernand; President Lincoln; General Fitz-John Porter; General McClellan; Joseph Camp Griffith Kennedy; Garrett (in light hat); Mather.

THE PRESIDENT AND GENERAL McCLELLAN

On the Battle-field of Antietam.

October 4, 1862.

Library of Congress O–66

LINCOLN BLUNTLY TELLS McCLELLAN that he wants a speedy advance against the enemy. The tenseness between the men is apparent as they sit in discussion, disdainful of the captured rebel flag which lies crumpled on the ground at the left. On the table is Lincoln's tall silk hat, flanked by two nearly gutted candles.

This photograph, like the others in the Antietam series, was probably taken by Gardner on October 3, but the enlargement published by Brady bears the printed date, October 4, 1862.

Head detail O–67A   Head detail O–

A QUERULOUS LOOK FOR GENERAL MCCLELLAN.   Lincoln sarcastically referred to the Army of the Potomac as "McClellan's bodyguard," and these two enlargements from the Gardner photographs of Lincoln in McClellan's tent show plainly the President's dissatisfaction with the overcautious General whom he was soon to relieve of his command. Enlarged for the first time from the original glass negative in the Library of Congress, the remarkable profile on the left reveals a half-smirk on the President's face as he stares at McClellan.

67A   O–67B

LINCOLN SITS PIGEON-TOED, hands in lap, in this second view of his conference with McClellan. Published in its entirety for the first time direct from the original glass negative plate in the Library of Congress, this stereograph was taken by Alexander Gardner, operator for Mathew Brady, Antietam, Maryland, Tuesday, October 3, 1862.

Lincoln as His Contemporaries Saw Him

Head detail O–74

"HIS EYE . . . is neither the quick sharp eye of a man of sudden and penetrating nature, nor the slow firm eye of one of decided will; but it is a mild, dreamy, meditative eye."

—Charles Francis Adams, Jr.

Head detail O–82

"THE MOUTH is absolutely prodigious; the lips, straggling and extending almost from one line of black beard to the other, are only kept in order by two deep furrows from the nostril to the chin."

—William Howard Russell, *London Times* reporter

O–112

"HIS EYES had an inexpressible sadness . . . with a far-away look, as if they were searching for something they had seen long, long years ago."

—Thomas Hicks, artist

114

Head detail   O–104

"HE WOULD RUN his fingers through his bristly black hair, which would stand out in every direction like that of an electric experiment doll."
—Benjamin Perley Poore

O–116

"HIS COMPLEXION is dark and sallow . . . he has thick black eyebrows . . . his nose is large . . . as coarse [a face] as you would meet anywhere . . . but redeemed, illuminated, softened, and brightened by a kindly though serious look . . . and an expression of homely sagacity."
—Nathaniel Hawthorne

Head detail   O–90

"NONE OF THE ARTISTS has caught the deep, though subtle and indirect expression, of this man's face. They have only caught the surface. There is something else there."   —Walt Whitman

Courtesy Douglas Gorsline O–68

Detail view O–68

"Daddy and Lincoln"

It was Lincoln's custom to visit the troops and chat informally with officers and men. Here he sits with soldiers of the Fifth New York Cavalry Regiment, known as the First Ira Harris Guard, a part of the army defending Washington from September, 1862, to February, 1863.

Never before published in a book, this photograph by O. Pierre Havens of Sing Sing, New York, was obtained from the descendants of Lieutenant Edmund Blunt, seated at the table on Lincoln's right. The Lieutenant wrote home that the President visited the regiment and "a photograph was made which included me." Thenceforth, the picture taken in Virginia between September, 1862, and February, 1863, was known to Blunt's family as "Daddy and Lincoln."

116

O–63   O–62   O–64

OUR TALLEST PRESIDENT—OUTDOORS.   "When standing straight and letting his arms fall down his sides," wrote Colonel Robert L. Wilson of Lincoln, ". . . his fingers would touch a point lower on his legs, nearly three inches, than was usual with other persons."

The soldier behind Lincoln is Captain (later General) George A. Custer. The band on the President's hat is in memory of his son Willie, who died in February, 1862.

All three poses were taken by Alexander Gardner at Antietam, Maryland, on Friday, October 3, 1862.

117

O–69

O–75

TAKEN AT BRADY'S,
April 17, 1863

TAKEN BY GARDNER,
August 9, 1863

OUR TALLEST PRESIDENT—STANDING INDOORS. "When I get all the kinks out," said Lincoln to Humphrey W. Carr of New Jersey, "I am six feet four inches." But according to the measurement taken by artist Frank Carpenter, the President stood six feet, three and three-fourths inches in his stocking feet.

O–94

Restored O–102

TAKEN BY BERGER,
February 9, 1864

TAKEN BY BERGER
at Brady's, April 26, 1864

L. C. Handy collection

BRADY UNDER FIRE.   Wearing a linen duster and a flat straw hat, Brady poses with soldiers at Petersburg [left]. The original photograph, entitled "Brady under fire," is from the L. C. Handy collection in Washington.

Ostendorf collection

MATHEW B. BRADY, the man with the "whatizzit" wagon, as the soldiers called the portable darkroom, was a familiar sight in the Union Army camps. A hurriedly scrawled "Pass Brady" signed by Lincoln took the noted cameraman or any of his twenty assistants wherever the troops marched, in bivouac or in action.

Ostendorf collection

BRADY'S WASHINGTON GALLERY. Often visited by Lincoln, it still stands, now occupied by the Gilman Prescription Drug firm.

BRADY OFTEN RISKED HIS LIFE and finally sacrificed his personal fortune to make a complete photographic history of the Civil War. He took the pictures of Bull Run; his assistant, Alexander Gardner, was with the Army of the Potomac; and Timothy O'Sullivan was at Gettysburg. All told, Brady and his men took more than 3,500 photographs.

BRADY ABOUT 1875. The man with the most famous by-line of his era, "Photograph by Brady," lost more than $100,000 in photographing the Civil War. He died in poverty in 1896.

L. C. Handy collection

121

CURIOUSLY, the man who took more pictures of Lincoln than any other photographer was camera-shy, for no studio portrait of Gardner is known. This picture, possibly based on a camera study, is from an oil painting discovered by Josephine Cobb of the National Archives.

ALEXANDER GARDNER, a former journalist who came from Glasgow in 1856 to join Brady's firm, was an expert in the Scott Archer wet-plate or collodion process, the advanced method of photography which by 1861 had almost entirely supplanted earlier processes. As manager of Brady's Washington gallery, Gardner followed the Army of the Potomac during the early years of the war, taking hundreds of pictures, his specialty being stereographs of battle and camp views. When Brady could no longer pay his salary, Gardner established his own gallery on the corner of Seventh and D streets in Washington.

Library of Congress

LINCOLN WAS THE FIRST SITTER at Gardner's Washington gallery. The signs advertise cartes-de-visite, stereographs, album cards, imperial photographs (plain, colored, and retouched), ambrotypes, hallotypes, and ivory types.

Ostendorf collection (

A STEREO CARD (O–49) produced by uniting images B and C taken by a multiple-lens camera. Published in 1864 by E. & H. T. Anthony & Co., No. 2969, in a series entitled "Prominent Portraits."

CONTEMPORARY THREE-DIMENSIONAL PORTRAITS. Only about six stereographs of Lincoln were published during his lifetime. They bear a publication date not later than 1865. With the exception of the outdoor views of Lincoln at Antietam, which were taken with a standard stereoscopic or two-lens camera, all of the contemporary published stereographs of the President were made by combining two of the images simultaneously recorded by a three- or four-lens camera.

In 1864 and 1865 the E. & H. T. Anthony Company published four different pairs of President Lincoln on their "Portrait Gallery" stereograph cards (O–49, O–84, O–103, and O–104). Their identification number, either "2968" or "2969," was given to all four views.

erican Antiquarian Society O-65

THE ONLY STEREO card published during Lincoln's lifetime (1862) which was actually taken with a stereoscopic camera. The photographer, Alexander Gardner, took
another stereo photograph at the same time (Lincoln and McClellan in the tent,
O-67), but it was not published as a stereo card until many years after the war in a
series entitled "Photographic War History, 1861-65."

Lincoln National Life Foundation   O–71

A UNIQUE STEREO CARD published by Alexander Gardner in 1864.

Ostendorf collection   O–84

AN EXTREMELY RARE stereo card (images C and D) published in 1864 by E. & H. T. Anthony & Co., No. 2968. Only two examples are known.

HON. ABRAHAM LINCOLN, President of United States.

American & Foreign

Portrait Gallery.

ibrary of Congress O–103

ANOTHER UNIQUE STEREO CARD, the only surviving example of which is in the Library of Congress. The recent discovery of upper image B proves that this card, long considered a true three-dimensional photograph, was actually made up by images C and D of a four-view plate taken by a multiple-lens camera. Usually attributed to Brady, this carte-de-visite photograph may have been taken by E. & H. T. Anthony & Co. (predecessors of Ansco) in 1865. Their imprint appears on this view as well as on their stereograph of a similar pose (O–104). An exact reprint was issued of O–103 many years after the war by the Keystone View Company.

O–69A

A Frenchman with a decided accent, Brady's operator, Thomas Le Mere, told Lincoln that there was a "considerable call" for a full-length standing photograph of him.

"Can it be taken with a single negative?" asked Lincoln, jesting.

After Le Mere's reassurance, the President explained that he had seen a very wide landscape photograph which, on inspection, proved to be a neatly joined series of photographs. "I thought perhaps this method might be necessary for my full-length landscape."

The carefully posed photograph opposite (O–69A), an enlargement from the original glass negative, was taken with a multiple-lens camera by Le Mere at Brady's gallery in Washington on or about Friday, April 17, 1863. When Lincoln saw the uncut glass negative, he exclaimed: "They look about as alike as three peas!"

To an early acquaintance, Lincoln penned a facetious reference to his height: "Don't you remember a long black fellow who rode on horseback with you from Tremont to Springfield . . . ?"

Meserve collection O–69A   Ostendorf collection O–69B   Lincoln Memorial University O–69C

LINCOLN POSES IN GARDNER'S NEW GALLERY on Sunday, August 9, 1863. Reproduced from a sepia enlargement, this is one of a series of six pictures of the President taken by Gardner on the day before the official opening of his gallery. Lincoln had promised to be Gardner's first sitter and chose Sunday for his visit to avoid "curiosity-seekers and other seekers" while on his way to the gallery.

GARDNER USED TWO CAMERAS, a regular single-lens instrument and a multiple-lens camera which exposed four images simultaneously, two upper and two lower, on a single large glass plate. Although each pair was stereoscopically related, this was incidental to the photographer, whose purpose was to make duplicates quickly and cheaply. Only one operation was needed to turn out four carte-de-visite photographs. The glass images were usually cut apart—no entire four-plate photograph of Lincoln is known to exist—and were then distributed to branches or assistants to insure maximum production.

Courtesy George Eastman House, Rochester, New York

AN ORIGINAL FOUR-LENS CAMERA

Lincoln Museum,
Old Ford's Theatre Building   O–71 c

TAKEN WITH A FOUR-LENS CAMERA.   Photograph (enlargement) by Alexander Gardner, Washington, August 9, 1863.

Lincoln National
Life Foundation   O–71A

Meserve collection   O–71B

Lincoln Museum   O–71C

From original negative,
Brown University Library   O–71D

PRECISELY HOW THE IMAGES APPEARED on the original plate may be seen from these pictures, assembled for the first time by Lloyd Ostendorf. The lower left pose C of the glass negative was discovered in 1934 in a collection left to Samuel Porter, whose father had operated a gallery in Washington.

There is a slightly different camera angle in each pose, especially obvious at the point where Lincoln's knee and coat seem to touch the table.

THE PRESIDENT LOOKS UP FROM HIS READING, spectacles in hand—an Alexander Gardner photograph taken in Washington on Sunday, August 9, 1863. Lincoln's secretary, John Hay, wrote in his diary of this sitting: "I went down with the President to have his picture taken at Gardner's. He was in very good spirits."

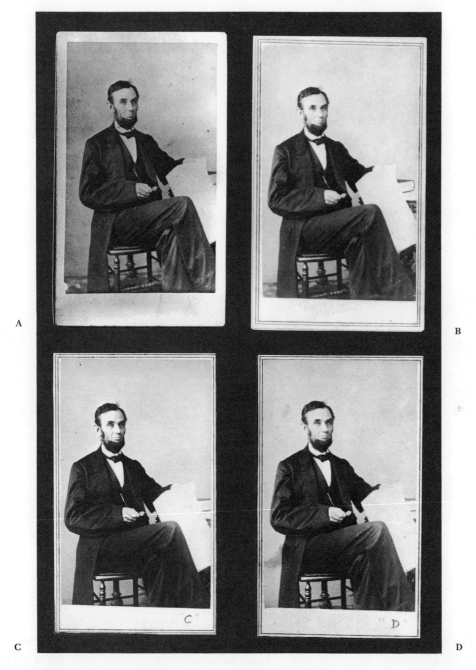

A

B

C

D

Ostendorf collection O–72

FOUR CARTE-DE-VISITE PHOTOGRAPHS, reassembled with horizontal images transposed to show the proper stereo relationship of each pair of views in the original multiple-lens plate. The variation in camera angle may again be seen at Lincoln's knee.

Ostendorf collection O–73 A

PHOTOGRAPH TAKEN WITH A FOUR-LENS CAMERA by Alexander Gardner, Washington, Sunday, August 9, 1863. The two images on the next page form an irregular half of a four-view plate, evidenced by the variant width of the ellipse formed by the table-top, for the upper lens naturally shows more of the table surface than the lower lens. A small section of missing image C is visible at the extreme left of image D, where the separation of the glass plate is apparent and the table design starts to be repeated.

Ostendorf collection   O–73 A

Missing view B

Missing view C

Meserve collection   O–73 D

FIRST FULL-LENGTH PUBLICATION. Photograph by Alexander Gardner, Washington, D. C., Sunday, August 9, 1863. The far-away look on the President's face recalls the comment of Gilbert Finch, an Alton Railroad conductor who knew Lincoln: "Sometimes I would see what looked like dreadful loneliness in his look, and I used to wonder what he was thinking about. Whatever it was he was thinking alone."

LINCOLN'S "PHOTOGRAPHER'S FACE". Whenever Lincoln posed, a dark melancholy settled over his features. He put on what Mrs. Lincoln called his "photographer's face." There is no camera study which shows him laughing, for such an attitude, unfortunately, was impossible when long exposures were required. A man who knew Lincoln, Dr. James Miner, commented: "His large bony face when in repose was unspeakably sad and as unreadable as that of a sphinx, his eyes were as expressionless as those of a dead fish; but when he smiled or laughed at one of his own stories or that of another then everything about him changed; his figure became alert, a lightning change came over his countenance, his eyes scintillated and I thought he had the most expressive features I had ever seen on the face of a man."

A CROPPED AND HIGHLY RETOUCHED VIEW, originally published as Meserve–55.

Meserve collection   Variant O–74

HE TOWERS ABOVE THE HEAD CLAMP. Photograph by Alexander Gardner, Washington, D. C., Sunday, August 9, 1863. Visible behind Lincoln's legs are the tips of the iron stander which supports the rod holding the head clamp, or "immobilizer," designed to keep the subject motionless during the exposure. A draped box about a foot high was placed under the stander to lift the immobilizer to the President's six-foot, four-inch height!

When Andrew D. White of New York visited Lincoln at the White House, he noted the President's "rather dusty suit of black," adding that he looked like "some rural tourist who had blundered into the place."

Missing view B

Meserve collection   O–75 A

Missing view C

Library of Congress   O–75 D

PUBLISHED TOGETHER for the first time, these two images from a four-lens photograph show that Lincoln appears taller from the angle of the lower lens. The A negative was originally discarded because of a defect and was not published until February, 1939, at which time it was in the collection of William Randolph Hearst.

WITH HIS PRIVATE SECRETARIES, Nicolay and Hay. Photograph by Alexander Gardner, Washington, Sunday, November 8, 1863. On this day John Hay wrote in his diary: "Went with Mrs. Ames to Gardner's Gallery & were soon joined by Nico [John G. Nicolay] and the Prest. We had a great many pictures taken . . . some of the Prest. the best I have seen. . . . Nico & I immortalized ourselves by having ourselves done in a group with the Prest." Years later the White House correspondent Noah Brooks, writing from memory, mistakenly ascribed this sitting to November 15, five days before the Gettysburg address.

Ostendorf collection   Detail O–76

DETAIL FROM AN UNRETOUCHED ENLARGEMENT by Gardner, with an excellent view of the left, seldom-photographed side of Lincoln's face. Gardner also published another face detail, vignetted and retouched.

143

FIRST PUBLICATION OF THE ENTIRE PHOTOGRAPH by Alexander Gardner, Washington, D. C., Sunday, November 8, 1863. From an original Gardner enlargement.

Ostendorf collection Head detail O–77

HIS "ROVING" LEFT EYE IS PLAINLY VISIBLE.   The dramatic power of this camera study is enhanced by its intimacy. The firm but irregular set of the lips and the cavernous depth of the eye-sockets with the upward roll of the left eye add to its impact.

145

THE FAMOUS "BIG FOOT" PHOTOGRAPH by Alexander Gardner, Washington, D. C., Sunday, November 8, 1863. The size of Lincoln's boots was joked about by his friends and ridiculed by his political opponents. They claimed that the President wore shoes a foot and a half in length.

146

THE GANGLING LEGS AND HUGE FEET of the President always created interest. A fifteen-year-old youth named Charles W. Nickum watched Tom Cridland take Lincoln's picture in Dayton and commented years later: "He was so long-legged that when he crossed one over the other, both feet seemed to rest on the floor."

The "big foot" photograph aroused Lincoln's curiosity: "I can understand why that foot should be so enormous," he said to Noah Brooks. "It's a big foot anyway, and it is near the focus of the instrument. But why is the outline of it so indistinct and blurred? I am confident I did not move it."

Brooks suggested that the throbbing of the arteries may have caused an imperceptible motion.

The President crossed his legs and watched his foot. "That's it! That's it!" he exclaimed. "Now that's very curious, isn't it?"

Only ten days after this sitting, Lincoln delivered his famous Gettysburg address. Near his right hand, on the table, is a white envelope containing an advance newspaper printing of the companion address at Gettysburg by Edward Everett.

Stereo pair from Ostendorf collection   O–78A and B

THIS INTERESTING PAIR possesses some stereo quality.

Henry Ford Museum, Dearborn, Michigan O-79

PHOTOGRAPH BY ALEXANDER GARDNER, Washington, D. C., November 8, 1863, also issued as a large vignette or an entire rectangle by Philp & Solomons of Washington. This enlargement emphasizes Lincoln's long, lanky legs. The elegant studio chair, called a "Brady chair," was discarded from the House of Representatives when it proved too narrow for the rotund congressmen.

LINCOLN'S POWERFUL SHOULDERS AND ARMS are shown in this first publication
of the entire photograph by Alexander Gardner, Washington, November 8,
1863. Reproduced direct from an original, uncropped sepia or gold-wash print.

THE BATTLEFIELD OF GETTYSBURG. It inspired the most famous address in history. "From these honored dead we take increased devotion to that cause for which they gave the last full measure of devotion . . . ."

—Abraham Lincoln.

151

LINCOLN RODE IN THIS PARADE. On the morning of November 19, 1863, along Baltimore Street in the little village of Gettysburg, huge crowds assembled to welcome the President. At ten o'clock the parade of dignitaries and soldiers began moving down the main avenue toward the cemetery which was to be dedicated. Lincoln was astride a large sorrel horse.

THE CEMETERY GATE AT GETTYSBURG. From a photograph taken in 1863.

ALTHOUGH SKILLFULLY ORGANIZED by Ward Hill Lamon, the procession was held up for an hour. The President remained patiently on horseback while the throngs gleefully shouted, "Hurrah for Old Abe!" and sang, "We are coming, Father Abraham." Then the parade marched across the battlefield where only four months earlier Lee had been turned back and the fate of the Confederacy decided. The marks of the terrible fight were still present, and the Indian-summer air was heavy with the odor of decay from the bodies of unburied horses.

Fabian Bachrach collection

THE CROWD AWAITS LINCOLN'S ADDRESS.   In the distance is the speaker's stand, at the right of which rises a tall flagpole. Because the flag was waving during the exposure, it was much blurred and had to be retouched by the cameraman, David Bachrach. When he sent the photograph to Lloyd Ostendorf (September, 1960), Louis Fabian Bachrach, Sr., wrote: "My father did not get a picture of Lincoln, and was only acting as assistant to the photographer of *Leslie's Weekly* at that time."

154

National Archives

THE ENTRANCE ARCH to Gettysburg Cemetery is visible near the top left of this view. In the huge crowd were several photographers, probably including Alexander Gardner and the Tyson brothers of Gettysburg. Mathew Brady was in New York, but he sent one of his cameramen.

So VAST WAS THE MULTITUDE that many, unable to get within hearing distance of the speakers, wandered over the battlefield in every direction.

National Archives

THE STACKED ARMS ARE SYMBOLIC.   A third view of the battlefield on which nearly six thousand young Americans gave their lives. On this warm Sunday afternoon the new national cemetery is crowded with spectators, one of whom has turned to stare into the camera!

The most-experienced photographers in America were present when Lincoln delivered his Gettysburg address. They brought their finest equipment. They had set up their cameras, lenses trained on the speaker's stand, hours before the dignitaries arrived. They were intent upon making a pictorial record of an important news event—the dedication of a great national memorial by the President.

Why, then, is there no close-up photograph of Lincoln making his speech?

The President was invited to give "a few appropriate remarks" after the noted diplomat, Edward Everett, had delivered the chief oration. In a two-hour talk freighted with baroque sentences and flowery adjectives, Everett spoke of the war and its heroes. The cameramen took no close-up picture of him or of the celebrities on the speaker's stand. They were waiting for Lincoln, whose remarks, as he had indicated to Noah Brooks ten days before, were to be "short, short, short."

Introduced by Ward Hill Lamon, the bespectacled President rose, drew several bits of paper from his coat pocket, shuffled them for a moment, and walked to the rostrum. There was a hush. Many in the crowd could hear the creaking of the boards under his feet. Some of them remembered that a cameraman began focusing his instrument.

In a high tenor voice, the President addressed a silent audience. The people were studying the gnarled features of this strange, tall man from the West, scarcely hearing his words, which came slowly, very slowly, as if Lincoln were doling them out to make them last as long as possible.

Then suddenly it was over! The photographer, still busy adjusting his camera, had taken no picture.

Later Lincoln observed that his talk "fell on the audience like a wet blanket." Some newspapers ignored it; others criticized it. But there was praise, too—high praise. A fifteen-year-old boy, George D. Gitt, heard the speech from a position directly under the President. He recalled that when the speaker "came to 'gave the last full measure of devotion,' tears trickled down Lincoln's cheeks, and I could not help some welling up in my own eyes." Another listener was the artist Freeman Thorpe. "We were all so astounded by his masterly phraseology and ideas that we could no more applaud it than we could, if present in the hottest part of the Gettysburg battle, have clapped our hands at the unyielding stand or heroic charge . . . of our army."

The brevity of Lincoln's address did not catch Brady's cameraman entirely unprepared. He had already taken the picture of the waiting speakers which appears on the next page.

National Archives O–

THE SPEAKER'S STAND is in the distance. Photograph, probably by an assistant of Mathew B. Brady, Gettysburg, Pennsylvania, November 19, 1863. Improperly labeled in the government archives as "Crowd of Citizens & Soldiers, etc.," this glass negative from the Brady collection was in 1953 tentatively identified as a view of Gettysburg by Josephine Cobb, chief of the Still-Photo Section of the National Archives. She correctly surmised that Lincoln was in the group, at the speaker's stand under the flag.

Ostendorf collection   Detail O–81

LINCOLN IS ABOUT TO DELIVER ten short sentences which will immortalize the Battle of Gettysburg. In the center of this unretouched enlargement the President stands hatless, head slightly bowed, with a small portion of his chin and beard obscured by a soldier's hat. At his left is Major General Robert C. Schenck. Edward Everett is at the far right, his face blurred, with hand on hip.

159

Osborn H. Oldroyd collection, Lincoln Museum   O–82 A

A CRAFTY AND DETERMINED PRESIDENT photographed by Lewis E. Walker, Washington, D. C., about 1863. Observe the almost casual attire, with the unbuttoned coat and the familiar watch chain hanging from the side pocket instead of the vest. The only personal ornament worn by Lincoln in any photograph is a watch chain. This heavy chain of hair-thin braided gold was presented to him in 1863 by a California delegation.

TAD MIMICS HIS FATHER (left) in this candid picture taken in Philadelphia about 1863 or 1864 and published here through the courtesy of Richard T. Gumpert.

A REASSEMBLED STEREO PORTRAIT (below). The image at the lower left (O–82 A) is from the only known carte-de-visite print. The right side of the glass plate (O–82 B) is slightly defective. It is published here for the first time from the collodion negative in the Ostendorf collection. Originally the plate belonged to Pearson Snyder Clime, a drummer boy from Pennsylvania. Possibly it was presented to Clime by the cameraman, Lewis E. Walker, a government photographer in the office of the Supervising Architect of the Capitol and the Supervising Architect of the Treasury Department.

Ostendorf collection   O–82 B

Lincoln Museum   O–82 A

Missing view A

B

C

Missing view D

A NEWLY DISCOVERED FOUR-LENS PORTRAIT. View O–85 B from the Meserve collection has long been familiar to Lincoln students. View O–85 C, a much finer picture, was discovered by Lloyd Ostendorf late in 1961 and is now in his collection.

162

Ostendorf collection O–85c

THE ODD LUMP ON HIS LOWER LIP is visible in this vignette photograph by Mathew B. Brady, Washington, D. C., Friday, January 8, 1864. The entire photograph, one of a series of five taken by Brady on January 8, 1864, has never come to light. Made with a four-lens camera, as were the other poses on the same day, it is quite different from the similar portrait on the following page (O–83). In comparing them, notice the entirely different expression, the wave in the hair, and the space between the collar and neck.

Lower left, Meserve collection; *others*, National Archives O–83

THIS MULTIPLE-LENS PHOTOGRAPH BY BRADY, taken at the sitting of January 8, 1864, has been reassembled from three separate collodion negatives. Images A, B, and D are from a contemporary collodion plate in the National Archives; C is from the glass negative in the Meserve collection.

164

National Archives O–83 D

THIS MAGNIFICENT PORTRAIT, an enlargement of image D from the four-lens plate, shows that Brady had a special process for copying glass or collodion negatives so that the duplicate plate could not be distinguished from the original. This photograph was reproduced from a contemporary plate, as was the identical image opposite (O–83 D), yet they were made from two separate glass negatives, for the scratches and defects are noticeably different.

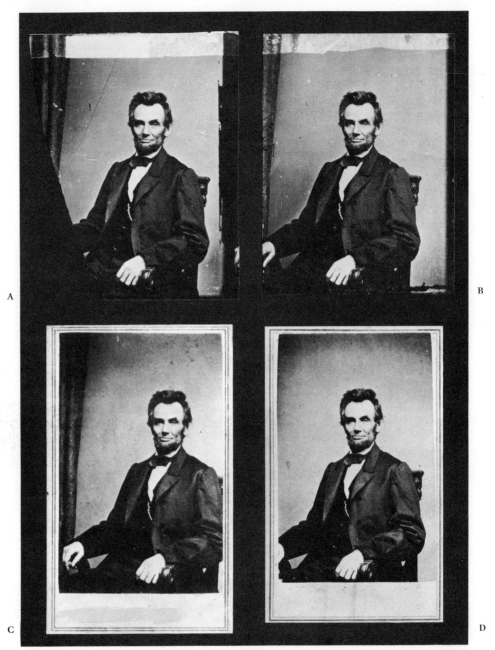

Top pair, National Archives; *bottom pair*, Ostendorf collection   O–84

A REASSEMBLED MULTIPLE-LENS PHOTOGRAPH by Mathew B. Brady, Washington, D. C., Friday, January 8, 1864. The National Archives owns *two* sets of glass negatives of images A and B, but no negatives for the lower pair, which are here united from carte-de-visite photographs in the Ostendorf collection. The difference in camera angle between the upper and lower pair is clear from the variation in size of the small opening under Lincoln's left coat sleeve.

166

National Archives O–84A

A FORMAL PORTRAIT BY BRADY taken at the sitting of Friday, January 8, 1864.
This enlargement is from a second negative, identical with O–84A (opposite),
but in better condition.

National Archives O–86A   National Archives O–86B

TWO IMAGES ON AN OLD COLLODION PLATE by Brady, January 8, 1864. As no matching images have turned up, it is possible that only the upper or lower half of the four-image glass plate was actually exposed. Images A and B show a three-dimensional quality when viewed through a stereoscope; but on the contemporary negative in the National Archives there is a third horizontal image, an exact repetition of image A on the right of image B. It shows no stereoscopic relief with the center image B, thus indicating that it was duplicated solely to speed up the printing of cartes-de-visite.

National Archives O–86B

"LIKE SOME SOLITARY PINE." The perspective in this enlargement of the magnificent portrait by Brady (January 8, 1864) calls to mind the comment of Francis Grierson that Lincoln "rose from his seat, stretched his long, bony limbs upward as if to get them into working order and stood like some solitary pine on a lonely summit."

Ostendorf collection   O–87c

LINCOLN LIKED THIS PHOTOGRAPH, taken with a multiple-lens camera by Math-ew B. Brady, Washington, D. C., Friday, January 8, 1864. He said of it: "I don't know that I have any favorite portrait of myself; but I have thought that if I looked like any of the likenesses of me that have been taken, I look most like that one."

170

Ostendorf collection   O–87

A PAIR OF STEREOGRAPHS reconstructed from cartes-de-visite. The negatives of the A and D images were partially opaqued for use as vignette portraits; the B and C images were left untouched and printed as waist-length pictures. The location of the original plates is unknown.

Meserve collection   O–88c

"THE FAMOUS PROFILE" by Anthony Berger, manager of Brady's Gallery, Washington, D. C., made direct from an original collodion negative in the Meserve collection (M–82). One of seven poses taken by Berger on Tuesday, February 9, 1864, it is perhaps the most familiar of Lincoln profiles, a more handsome pose than its companion view (O–89) because Lincoln's profile is less severe and his left eyebrow is more visible. Notice the difference in the sleeve wrinkles in O–88D and O–89C.

A

B

Ostendorf collection   O–88

A NEWLY DISCOVERED vignetted upper pair from the four-lens photograph by Berger.

C

D

Meserve collection   O–88

COMPLETE LOWER PAIR from separate original glass negatives in the Meserve collection, M–82 (left) and M–81 (right), these handsome portraits make a splendid stereographic view. This is the first publication of the reconstructed four-image plate.

Meserve collection O–89c

THE PENNY PROFILE. Photograph by Anthony Berger, manager of Brady's Gallery, Washington, D. C., Tuesday, February 9, 1864. Perhaps Brady helped Berger position Lincoln for the seven poses taken at this sitting. In 1909 the artist Victor D. Brenner used this and the preceding profile (O–88) to model the Lincoln-head cent.

174

A

B

Upper pair, Ostendorf collection; *lower left*, Meserve collection   O–89

Missing view D

C

UPPER VIGNETTED IMAGES (top) from carte-de-visite photographs. Complete view from an original plate (bottom). The President walked more than a mile for this sitting. In his unpublished diary, artist Frank B. Carpenter recorded that Lincoln, impatient during a long wait for his carriage, said: "I guess we will walk on and not wait. . . . I don't think it will hurt me a bit to walk; I'm pretty much split up for our having had to wait like this!"

Ostendorf collection   O-92

"THE MOST SATISFACTORY LIKENESS."   Photograph by Anthony Berger, Brady Gallery, Washington, D. C., Tuesday, February 9, 1864. Thirty years after his father's death, Robert T. Lincoln wrote to Meserve: "I have always thought the Brady photograph of my father, of which I attach a copy, to be the most satisfactory likeness of him."

176

THE FAMOUS OVAL PORTRAIT adapted from the photograph of Lincoln on the opposite page and engraved on the five-dollar bill.

A WIDELY CIRCULATED carte-de-visite photo-copy (lower right) of an engraved portrait based on Berger's camera study, often mistaken for a print of the original photograph.

Artist Frank B. Carpenter, to whom Lincoln later gave a special camera sitting, was evidently present when Berger took the seven photographs in this series. On the back of a cabinet photograph (O–92) with Brady's imprint, he wrote:

"From a negative made in 1864, by A. Berger, partner of M. B. Brady, at Brady's gallery. This is the photograph engraved by J. C. Butre of New York, just after Mr. Lincoln's re-nomination. It was the basis after Mr. Lincoln's death of the portrait made by Marshall, and also the one made by Littlefield. In each engraving the parting of the hair was changed, to the *left side*, as Mr. Lincoln always wore it. His barber by mistake this day for some unaccountable reason, parted the hair on the President's *right* side, instead of his *left*."

Ostendorf collection   Variant O–92
CARTE-DE-VISITE VARIANT

177

National Archives O–91

A PHOTOGRAPH WHICH INSPIRED MANY PAINTINGS. Photograph by Anthony Berger, Brady's Gallery, Washington, D. C., Tuesday, February 9, 1864. An original, cracked plate in the National Archives measures 14¼ inches by 17⅝ inches, just under the size known as "imperial."

Ostendorf collection   O–91

Ostendorf collection

A COMMON engraved carte-de-visite variant of the original portrait by Berger. It is often mistaken for a new photograph.

A STRIKING HEAD-DETAIL enlargement of the photograph opposite reveals Lincoln with just a faint suggestion of merriment in his sparkling eyes, as though a smile were about to ignite his masklike features.

A

B

Missing view D

C

Top images, National Archives; *lower left*, Meserve collection   O–90

MULTIPLE-LENS PHOTOGRAPH by Anthony Berger, Brady Gallery, Washington, D. C., Tuesday, February 9, 1864. These three stereoscopically related images show that Berger used a four-lens camera. In the National Archives is an old glass negative on which views A and B appear, with a third image (not shown here), an exact repetition of A. Stefan Lorant advanced the theory that the cameraman made three different, very quick-time exposures, moving a single-lens plateholder while the President remained motionless. But the stereo relationship of images A and B disproves this idea and suggests that the collodion negative was probably a copy plate used for mass reproduction.

National Archives O–90 B

THE BACK OF THIS RARE COLLODION PLATE in the National Archives was originally partially opaqued, with only the head and shoulders untouched. When
Lloyd Ostendorf removed the tape and varnish from image A, the entire picture, including the left hand of Lincoln, was visible for the first time.

LINCOLN AND TAD STUDY A BRADY ALBUM in this photograph by Anthony Berger, Brady's Gallery, Washington, D. C., Tuesday, February 9, 1864. One of the most popular Lincoln portraits, this is the only close-up of him wearing spectacles. It was issued in huge quantities in many variations, with and without Brady's permission.

Ostendorf collection O–93 A   F. Ray Ridson collection (M–127) O–93 B

THIS RARE STEREOGRAPHIC PAIR, published together for the first time, show that Berger used a multi-lens camera, vignetting the left image for artistic effect.

Meserve collection (M–39)
Variant O–93
RETOUCHED "BIBLE" VARIANT

LINCOLN OBSERVED TO NOAH BROOKS that the large volume with brass clasps (which also appears in photograph O–92) looked pretty much like a Bible. The President was apprehensive that the picture might be looked upon as "a species of false pretense . . . whereas it was a big photograph album which the photographer, posing the father and son, had hit upon as a good device . . . to bring the two sitters together." Lincoln's honesty was not emulated by the unknown artist who retouched the scene (left) to change the album into a family Bible!

Lincoln National Life Foundation O–95

A WHITE HOUSE PHOTOGRAPH by Wenderoth
& Taylor (of Philadelphia), Washington, D.C.,
sometime in 1864. An advertisement by Wenderoth, Taylor and Brown in the *Philadelphia
Enquirer*, April 20, 1865, offered for sale "card
photographs in large or small quantities of
President Lincoln taken from life at the White
House." Oval variant (right), slightly retouched, has softer lines, shows vest, watch
chain, and winding key.

Lincoln Memorial University collection

Ostendorf collection O–96

A SECOND WHITE HOUSE photograph by Wenderoth & Taylor (of Philadelphia), Washington,
D. C., sometime in 1864. In this enlargement of a
carte-de-visite portrait, Lincoln has a pensive, almost dreamy expression. The "wrong-side" part
in his hair suggests that this picture, like those in
the sitting by Berger, was taken in February or
March of 1864. Variant (right) shows more of
Lincoln's shoulders.

Ostendorf collection   (M–80)
Variant O–96

185

CARPENTER'S LIFE PORTRAIT OF LINCOLN, 1864.
Engraved by F. Halpin. Based on
the privately commissioned series
of photographs by Anthony Berger.

LINCOLN POSES FOR FRANK B. CARPEN-
TER. On Sunday, November 29, 1863,
Carpenter wrote in his diary that he
had "conceived the idea of painting a
picture commemorative of the First
Reading in Cabinet council of the
Emancipation Proclamation by President Lincoln." The artist moved into
the White House, where he could observe the President. He needed some
photographs as a guide, and at his
request Lincoln sat several times for
Anthony Berger, manager of Brady's
Washington studio. The story is told
by Carpenter in these excerpts from
his unpublished diary:

Friday, Dec. 25th. . . . Mrs. Lincoln informed me that President Lincoln
would sit for my large picture of the "Reading of the Proclamation of Free-
dom to the Cabinet."

Feb. 9, 1864. Went to the President and sat with him and Judge Holt
during the morning in his study. . . . Got ambrotype of President at Brady's
this P.M.

Feb. 10, 1864. With the President this morning. After lunch had the first
short sitting from Mr. Lincoln.

Feb. 11, 1864. Worked upon the picture of Mr. Lincoln today. Got along
well.

Feb. 12, 1864 [Lincoln's fifty-fifth birthday]. Had second sitting from
Mr. Lincoln this P.M. . . . it is already a capital likeness . . . .

Feb. 23, 1864. Found that Berger at Brady's had made a picture of Mr.
Stanton in the position I told him to put him in . . . .

Wed., March 2nd. President Lincoln gave me a good sitting this P.M.

March 28th. Marked day! . . . stretched my large canvas . . . all ready to
begin the painting in earnest . . . .

Tuesday, April 26, 1864. Today, Mr. Berger took several pictures for
me of Mr. Lincoln in the Cabinet room. Succeeded very well!

Courtesy of Emerson Carpenter Ives O–99

A CUT-OUT HEAD FROM A SCRAPBOOK. Photograph by Anthony Berger, Brady's Gallery, Washington, D. C., Wednesday, April 20, 1864. This portrait was privately taken for Frank B. Carpenter and unpublished during Lincoln's lifetime. The negative and the missing portion of the print were lost or destroyed.

187

Original negative, Ostendorf collection   O–97

THE "BROKEN PLATE" PHOTOGRAPH by Anthony Berger, Brady's Gallery,
Washington, D. C., Wednesday, April 20, 1864. Taken for artist Frank B.
Carpenter, this superb camera study brings to mind John G. Nicolay's remark
that "graphic art was powerless before a face that moved through a thousand
delicate gradations of line and contour, light and shade, sparkle of the eye and
curve of the lip."

Ostendorf collection (copyright, 1956)   O–98

AN UNPUBLISHED COMPANION PHOTOGRAPH by Anthony Berger, Brady's Gallery, Washington, D. C., Wednesday, April 20, 1864. This and the preceding view, reproduced from the original negatives, were given to Lloyd Ostendorf in 1955–56 by Carpenter's grandson, Emerson Carpenter Ives. In this imperfectly focused portrait, Lincoln's head is cocked slightly and turned more toward the viewer.

Courtesy of Emerson Carpenter Ives O-101

SEATED AT THE EMANCIPATION PROCLAMATION TABLE. Photograph by Anthony Berger of Brady's Gallery, White House Cabinet Room, Washington, D. C., Tuesday, April 26, 1864. Posed under the direction of Frank B. Carpenter, this and the following pictures show the difficulty of indoor photography under poor lighting conditions. The President's left arm rests on the table used for the signing of the Emancipation Proclamation. Behind him is his famous pigeon-hole desk, in one compartment of which he filed assassination threats.

Ostendorf collection O–100c

"SUCH LONG LEGS!" wrote New York businessman Benjamin F. Seaver. "They stick up in the air, as he sits in an ordinary chair." This multiple-lens photograph by Anthony Berger of Brady's Gallery, White House Cabinet Room, Washington, D. C., Tuesday, April 26, 1864, shows Lincoln's legs wider apart. The crossed legs in the light trousers are those of John G. Nicolay; the leg at the left is Carpenter's.

ALTHOUGH ONLY TWO IMAGES (shown on the next page) from this pose are known, they reveal that the photographer used four lenses. Notice that image A shows a small portion of the start of image B on the right edge; Carpenter's knee and leg appear twice in the picture, which indicates that the pose was repeated. The table-top is broader in the upper view because of the higher angle of the lens.

Later Carpenter told an amusing story about this sitting: "Some photographers from Brady's Gallery came up to the White House to make some stereoscopic studies for me of the President's office. They requested a dark closet, in which to develop the pictures; I took them to an unoccupied room . . . which little Tad had . . . fitted up as a miniature theatre. . . . one or two pictures had been taken, when suddenly there was an uproar. The operator came back to the office and said that Tad had taken great offence at the occupation of his room without his consent, and had locked the door, refusing all admission. The chemicals had been taken inside and there was no way of getting at them, he having carried off the key. . . .

ENLARGED DETAIL.   The light from the window of the Cabinet Room gives Rembrandt-like contrasts to Lincoln's face.

"Mr. Lincoln had been sitting for a photograph, and was still in the chair. He said, very mildly, 'Tad, go and unlock the door.' "

Refusing, Tad ran out of the room in anger. His father followed, and soon returned with the key. He then personally opened the door of the improvised darkroom.

A

Missing view B

Missing view D

C

Top, courtesy of Emerson Carpenter Ives; *bottom*, Ostendorf collection   O–100

THE FACELESS PHOTOGRAPH by Anthony Berger of Brady's Gallery, White House Cabinet Room, Washington, D. C., Tuesday, April 26, 1864. Carpenter noted on the back of an original print that this picture was taken under his direction. Possibly the face was accidentally smudged when Tad locked the darkroom.

Ostendorf collection O–102

THE FACELESS PHOTOGRAPH RESTORED

LINCOLN WITH A CREW-CUT!   Multiple-lens photograph, probably by the E. &
H. T. Anthony Co., Washington, D. C., about February, 1865. The President's
hair is cropped so close that it stands almost straight up, giving him a startled
look. "His hair was every way for Sunday," commented Henry Ward Beecher.
"It looked as though it was an abandoned stubble field."

Library of Congress O–103 A   Ostendorf collection O–103 B

THE LOWER VIEWS of this four-lens camera portrait were enlarged and published as a stereograph by E. & H. T. Anthony Co. in 1865. A multiple-lens instrument, rather than a stereoscopic camera, was used for this pose, in which Lincoln's hair, to quote artist Alban Jasper Conant, stands out "like an oven broom."

rary of Congress O–103 C and D

THE SHORT HAIRCUT was perhaps suggested by Lincoln's barber to facilitate the taking of his life mask by Clark Mills. Lincoln knew from experience how long hair could cling to plaster.

Ostendorf collection   O–104A and B

An 1865 STEREOGRAPH long attributed to Mathew B. Brady or Thomas Walker, this portrait of the President probably was taken about February, 1865, by a cameraman from the E. & H. T. Anthony Co., New York photographers whose imprint appears on their 1865 carte-de-visite and stereograph prints. The Anthony firm may have sent an operator to Washington, D. C., to obtain this and the preceding picture (O–103), both of which were published as stereograph cards bearing the Anthony imprint. The extremely rare stereograph (O–104, above) was found in 1962. There are dark lines and shadows in Lincoln's face; his eyes are deep and sorrowful; his beard is grizzled. In October, 1864, he was visited by Mrs. Anna Byers-Jennings, who later wrote, "When I entered he raised his tired eyes, oh so tired, and with a worn look I can never forget."

Library of Congress

THE SECOND INAUGURAL.   Many of the spectators waiting in the early morning drizzle recalled the first inaugural, which had taken place on a bright, clear morning.

200

rtesy Barbara B. Benoit

THE NAME OF THE CAMERAMAN who took this unpublished side view is not known, but likely it and the preceding view were made by Henry F. Warren, who had come from Waltham, Massachusetts, determined not to leave Washington without a picture of the President.

Library of Congress O—

BELIEVED UNPUBLISHED. A rare photograph by an unknown cameraman, probably Gardner, taken at the east front of the Capitol Building, Washington, D. C., Saturday, March 4, 1865. Discovered by Lloyd Ostendorf in the files of the National Archives in February, 1962, this scene appears to be the earliest of the Second Inaugural views which shows Lincoln.

Library of Congress   Detail O-105

ENLARGED DETAIL.   Lincoln sits at left center, his white collar and starched white shirt plainly visible. The huge audience is restless, waiting for him to be introduced.

WALT WHITMAN WATCHED LINCOLN on the way to the Capitol Building: "He was in his plain two-horse barouche, and look'd very much worn and tired; the lines . . . of vast responsibilities, intricate questions, and demands of life and death, cut deeper than ever upon his dark brown face; yet all the old goodness, tenderness, sadness, and canny shrewdness, underneath the furrows . . . . By his side sat his little boy, of ten years."

THE CROWD AWAITS THE PRESIDENT'S ADDRESS.   In this photograph (O–106), similar to the scene on the preceding page, Lincoln still sits at left center, his white collar and shirt again clearly recorded by the camera. The people are beginning to settle down for one of the shortest—and greatest—inaugural addresses in history.

On Lincoln's left are the justices of the Supreme Court; on his right are the members of his cabinet. At his immediate right, seated with crossed legs, is Andrew Johnson; and, next to Johnson, looking towards the cameraman, is the outgoing Vice-President, Hannibal Hamlin. Lincoln is half-a-head taller than his running mates.

Taken at the east front of the Capitol Building, Washington, D. C., on Saturday, March 4, 1865, this view, possibly by Alexander Gardner, is from the Meserve collection.

205

NEGATIVE BY WM. M. SMITH.   POSITIVE BY A. GARDNER.

Re-Inauguration of President Lincoln,
4th March, 1865.

King V. Hostick, Chicago, Ill. O-107

A MAGNIFICENT NEW DISCOVERY is this striking distant view of Lincoln's second inaugural. It was found in San Francisco in the fall of 1962 by noted Lincoln expert King V. Hostick of Chicago and his associate Gene Snack.

206

ENLARGEMENT OF INAUGURAL SCENE. In this detail from the picture opposite (O–107) we see the indistinct figure of Lincoln, who stands behind the white table holding a printed copy of his address.

THE ONLY KNOWN FRONT VIEW of Lincoln's second inaugural, this picture was taken shortly after noon on Saturday, March 4, 1865. Although the figure of Lincoln is barely visible, the photograph has caught the pageantry of the inaugural, framing the scene with two lamp posts flanked on the right by Washington's statue. The view was taken by William Morris Smith, a cameraman and patent attorney who operated his own gallery in Washington but was also employed by Alexander Gardner.

The authors are deeply indebted to King V. Hostick for his generosity in foregoing his own publication plans to allow the inclusion here of this important photograph.

Ostendorf collection O-108

As LINCOLN SPEAKS, the sun breaks out. Photograph, probably by Alexander Gardner, east front of Capitol Building, Washington, D. C., Saturday, March 4, 1865. Neither Gardner nor Brady copyrighted any pictures of the inauguration, but this and other views are usually considered Gardner's work.

The newly found photograph opposite (O-109) was taken at the same time by an unknown cameraman. The detail enlargement reveals John Wilkes Booth, who was to kill Lincoln ten days later.

Ostendorf collection Detail O-108

ENLARGED DETAIL

208

Ostendorf collection O–109

WATCHING PANTHER-LIKE from the corner of his eye, Booth
stands almost within derringer range of the President and hears
him urge the people to "bind up the nation's wounds; to care
for him who shall have borne the battle, and for his widow, and
his orphan—to do all which may achieve and cherish a just and
lasting peace among ourselves." The figure of Lincoln is blurred
from his slight motion during the speech, but Booth stands out
in sharp focus behind the railed balcony above the President.
The actor wears a stovepipe hat, as does bearded John T. Ford,
owner of Ford's Theatre, directly in front of Booth. Some
authorities have identified the man in the broad-brimmed white
hat and Union jacket standing below and just to the right of
Lincoln's rostrum as Booth's accomplice, the Confederate de-
serter, Lewis Paine; but the focus does not permit positive identification and the costume tends to disprove the contention.

Ostendorf collection Detail O–109
LINCOLN AND BOOTH
Enlarged detail

209

Courtesy Emerson Carpenter Ives O–

THE SECOND INAUGURAL ADDRESS—FIRST PUBLICATION. Photograph, possibly by Alexander Gardner, east front of Capitol Building, Washington, D. C., Saturday, March 4, 1865. Lincoln's features are slightly retouched to give them more contrast to the background. A soldier observed that Lincoln's voice "was not heavy or coarse, but singularly clear and penetrating, with almost a metallic ring."

Courtesy Emerson Carpenter Ives Detail O–111

THIS DETAIL from the previously unpublished photograph formerly owned by Frank B. Carpenter shows the artist (in cape) standing only a few feet behind the President.

FRANK B. CARPENTER, photographed at Gardner's Gallery, Washington, D. C., in 1864.

211

LINCOLN HOLDS A SINGLE PAGE on which is printed his entire inaugural address. Photograph, probably by Gardner, east front of Capitol Building, Washington, D. C., Saturday, March 4, 1865. As the President kissed the Bible, affirming his oath of office, the sun burst forth like an omen of peace.

Reading from a galley proof of two broad columns on a single sheet, Lincoln delivers to a rapt audience one of the briefest and best known of Presidential inaugural addresses. Next to him, Andrew Johnson, slightly tipsy from a medicinal drink, shields his face from the sun with his top hat; John Hay stands behind the President's empty chair; on Lincoln's right sits Chief Justice Salmon P. Chase, followed by Associate Justices Wayne, Nelson, Clifford, Swayne, Miller, and Field. The blurred figure of Lincoln is retouched. Above him, Booth is visible under the arm of the statue on the railed balcony.

TAD LINCOLN. Original unpublished carte-de-visite by Henry F. Warren, Washington, D. C., Sunday, March 4 or 5, 1865.

TAD ON HIS PONY. Photograph probably by Henry F. Warren, Washington, D. C., March 4 or 5, 1865. Tad wears a different suit.

H. F. WARREN of Waltham, Massachusetts, wanted desperately to take a picture of Lincoln. He was not acquainted with the President and had no connections in Washington. But he had a plan. Warren found out that Tad went riding on his pony every afternoon about three. He "ambushed and shot" young Lincoln astride his pony and on the following afternoon delivered the prints to Tad. The boy was delighted with them.

"Now," said Warren, "bring out your father and I will make a picture of him for you."

Tad dashed off, and in a few minutes appeared on the south balcony of the White House with the President.

Ostendorf collection   O-112

TWO DAYS AFTER THE SECOND INAUGURAL, a photograph by Henry F. Warren, south balcony of the White House, late afternoon, Monday, March 6, 1865.

When Tad brought his father out on the balcony for the special sitting, the President carried his own chair. Warren took three pictures of Lincoln, two seated and one standing. The standing pose is lost, but the vignetted likeness (above) was widely circulated by Warren. Posing just to please his son, Lincoln appears preoccupied and perhaps a little annoyed at the method Warren used to get the sitting. It was windy on the balcony, and this portrait illustrates aptly the comment of William H. Herndon, Lincoln's law partner, that "his hair . . . lay floating where his fingers or the winds left it, piled up at random."

Ostendorf collection O–113

HIS FACE IS TIRED AND WORN. First book publication of a photograph by Henry F. Warren, south balcony of the White House, late afternoon, Monday, March 6, 1865.

A pose similar to the preceding, this expressive portrait shows the weary President with his chin higher, hair pattern changed, and with a slightly different expression. Among those who noted the weariness in Lincoln's face was Colonel Silas W. Burt of New York: "The drooping eyelids, looking almost swollen; the dark bags beneath the eyes; the deep marks about the large and expressive mouth; the flaccid muscles of the jaws, were all so majestically pitiful."

LINCOLN AS HE SAW HIMSELF. "If any personal description of me is thought desirable," wrote Lincoln during the 1860 campaign, "it may be said I am, in height, six feet four inches, nearly; lean in flesh, weighing on an average one hundred and eighty pounds; dark complexion, with coarse black hair and gray eyes. No other marks or brands recollected."

Lincoln often jested about his appearance. "In the matter of looks I have the advantage," he used to say, meaning that he felt sorry for those who had to look at him.

He explained his homeliness with the following tale: "When I was two months old I was the handsomest child in Kentucky, but my Negro nurse swapped me off for another boy, just to please a friend who was going down the river, whose child was rather plain-looking."

Once in his youth, so the story goes, Lincoln was stopped by a stranger who pointed his rifle at the future President. "Hold on," cried Lincoln, "what do you think you are doing?"

"I took a vow on the grave of my mother that if I ever met a homelier man than I, I'd shoot him!"

Lincoln looked him over for a second or two and observed, "Well, stranger, if I am any uglier looking than you, I think you'd better shoot me."

LINCOLN IN 1860

216

During the debates with Douglas, his rival called him two-faced. Retorted Lincoln: "I leave it to my audience. If I had another face, do you think I'd wear this one?"

The orders of President Lincoln often annoyed his brusque secretary of war, Stanton, who at last burst out, "We've got to get rid of that baboon at the White House!"

The remark was repeated to Lincoln. "Mr. President," added his informant, "I would not endure such an insult."

"Insult? insult?" queried Lincoln. "That is no insult. It is an expression of opinion. And what troubles me most about it is the fact that Stanton said it, and Stanton is usually right."

Said Lincoln to General Egbert L. Viele: "If I have one vice, it is not to be able to say no! Thank God," he went on, "for not making me a woman, but if He had, I suppose He would have made me just as ugly as He did, and no one would ever have tempted me."

1861 O–51

1862 O–59

O–77

1864 O–86

1865 O–114

217

THE LAST SITTING. As four years of bitter warfare ground to an end, Lincoln made a long trip to the front to look over his victorious fighting men and to talk with his generals. Horace Greeley noted that "his face was haggard with care and seamed with thought and trouble. It looked care-ploughed, tempest-tossed, and weatherbeaten." Lincoln told Grant that he wanted a merciful peace. On April 9 he returned to Washington, and that night came a telegram from Grant: "General Lee surrendered the Army of Northern Virginia this morning on terms proposed by myself."

The next morning an exhausted but tranquil Lincoln visited Alexander Gardner's gallery for what was to be his final sitting.

Library of Congress   (Enlargement) O-114

PHOTOGRAPH ENLARGEMENT by Alexander Gardner, Gardner's Gallery, Washington, D. C., Monday, April 10, 1865. An interesting view of Lincoln and Tad. One of five poses taken by Gardner four days before the President was assassinated.

Ostendorf collection   (Meserve–95)   O–114   Ostendorf collection   (Meserv

THE SYLVAN BACKGROUND in this portrait of Lincoln and Tad was added for artistic effect. Both the original pose (left) and the ornamented view (right) were sold by Gardner. Other photographs of the period, such as O–76 (Lincoln with his secretaries, Nicolay and Hay) and O–93 (Lincoln and Tad examining a Brady album) were also adorned with baroque settings.

AFTER FOUR YEARS OF WAR . . . two portraits in contrast. "The fidelity of the photograph," complained English historian Goldwin Smith after meeting Lincoln, "has given the features of the original, but left out the expression." If Smith's remark applies to many Lincoln portraits, such as the 1861 likeness (below, left) in which the new President's face is almost a mask, it certainly is not true of the magnificent pose (below, right) taken only four days before his murder. In the dark, tired, haggard Lincoln of 1865 there is a warmth which even the impersonal eye of the camera cannot fail to record.

Ostendorf collection   Detail O-51

AGE FIFTY-TWO, 1861

Ostendorf collection   Detail O-114

AGE FIFTY-SIX, 1865

Missing view A

B

C

D

All views from Ostendorf collection O–115

MULTIPLE-LENS PHOTOGRAPH by Alexander Gardner, Gardner's Gallery, Washington, D. C., Monday, April 10, 1865. Image C from an old proof print and image D from a carte photograph make a stereo pair.

Ostendorf collection   Enlargement of O-115c

HIS TIRED EYES ARE LOST IN SHADOWS.   Taken from Gardner's original proof print, this rare, full view shows Lincoln's hands.

223

A

B

C

D

Views A and D, Meserve collection; views B and C, Ostendorf collection O–116

MULTIPLE-LENS PHOTOGRAPH by Alexander Gardner, Gardner's Gallery, Washington, D. C., Monday, April 10, 1865. Reconstruction of all four images as they originally appeared on the now-lost collodion plate.

Ostendorf collection   Enlargement of O–116c

HIS GNARLED HANDS FIDGET during the last sitting. First publication of the entire photograph from Gardner's proof print. Lincoln's long right leg is grotesquely enlarged by the camera lens. The President holds his spectacles and a pencil, both blurred, showing that he moved his fingers nervously during the exposure.

Ostendorf collection   Variant O-116D

WITH PENCIL AND SPECTACLES RETOUCHED.   When the camera failed to record
some fascinating or intimate detail, the photographer often employed an artist
to retouch or add to the scene. Here Lincoln's spectacles and pencil, blurred in
the original negative, are plainly outlined. The clarity and brilliance of this
photograph suggests that it may be a print direct from the original quarter-plate
D, now lost.

Ostendorf collection   Variant O–116D

WITH PENCIL AND KNIFE ADDED—another variant. There is a story that during
the last sitting Lincoln took out his pocket-knife to sharpen a pencil for Tad.
The tale may be true, but the knife in this picture was added by an artist. The
clarity of this almost unretouched photograph, identical with the opposite picture, indicates that it also may be a print direct from the original collodion plate.

227

Missing view A

B

C

Missing view D

Ostendorf collection O–117

MULTIPLE-LENS PHOTOGRAPH by Alexander Gardner, Gardner's Gallery, Washington, D. C., Monday, April 10, 1865. This dignified pose recalls the epithet applied to Lincoln by scientist Joseph Henry—"a man whose honesty and purpose is transparent."

Ostendorf collection   Enlargement of O-117B

THE MASK HIDING LINCOLN'S INTENSE EMOTIONS has fallen away to reveal a man at peace with himself.

"Even when he was pensive or gloomy," wrote Noah Brooks, "his features were lighted up very much as a clouded alabaster vase may be softly illuminated by a light within."

229

Meserve collection O–41   New York Historical Society   Variant O–118

JANUARY 13, 1861   APRIL 10, 1865

THE FIRST AND LAST BEARDED PHOTOS.   When his whiskers first appeared, the public reaction was mixed. The beard gives "additional cadaverousness to his face," declared Noah Brooks. But Anna Ridgeway, who was being courted by Robert T. Lincoln, wrote in her diary that "Mr. Lincoln really looks handsome to me; his whiskers are a great improvement and he had such a pleasant smile I could not but admire him."

The retouched print of a variant of O–118 (right) was published under the imprint of "A. Gardner, Photographer, by Philp & Solomons, Publisher, Washington." The President's beard and sideburns are trimmed more closely than at any time since he entered the White House.

Meserve collection O-118

THE LAST PHOTOGRAPH FROM LIFE, by Alexander Gardner, Gardner's Gallery, Washington, D. C., Monday, April 10, 1865. After Gardner had taken several multiple-lens pictures of the President, he moved his camera closer for this final studio portrait. Symbolically, the glass plate cracked, and after a single print was made, the negative broke completely and Gardner threw it away.

There is a gentle smile on Lincoln's face, and his eyes seem fixed on some far horizon. In exactly fourteen days he will be photographed once more, for the last time, as he lies in his casket.

Smithsonian Institution

A BRONZE CASTING of the life mask by Clark Mills.

BECAUSE OF THE SUNKEN EYES and cadaverous
cheeks, the second life mask of Lincoln, made in
February, 1865, is often mistaken for a death
mask. The sculptor Clark Mills made the plaster
mask in about fifteen minutes, one-fourth of the
time which Volk had required in 1860. Mills
first put a tight cap over Lincoln's hair, then
spread wet plaster over his entire face and
greased whiskers. He left only the nostrils open.
After the plaster hardened, he told the President
to move his facial muscles. As the plaster worked
loose, pieces fell and the sculptor caught them in
a towel, later reuniting them in the privacy of
his studio.

CLARK MILLS, Washington sculp

232

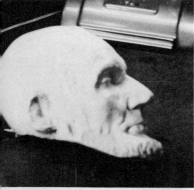

FOUR YEARS OF WAR, explained John Hay, who once owned Mills' original cast, had entirely altered Lincoln's face: "This change is shown with startling distinctness by two life-masks—the one made by Leonard W. Volk in Chicago, April, 1860 [page 64 above], the other by Clark Mills in Washington, in the spring of 1865. The first is of a man of fifty-one, and young for his years. The face has a clean, firm outline; it is free from fat, but the muscles are hard and full; the large mobile mouth is ready to speak, to shout, or laugh; the bold, curved nose is broad and substantial, with spreading nostrils; it is a face full of life, of energy, of vivid aspiration. The other is so sad and peaceful in its infinite repose that the famous sculptor Augustus Saint-Gaudens insisted, when he first saw it, that it was a death-mask. The lines are set, as if the living face, like the copy, had been in bronze; the nose is thin, and lengthened by the emaciation of the cheeks; the mouth is fixed like that of an archaic statue; a look as of one on whom sorrow and care had done their worst without victory is on all the features; the whole expression is of unspeakable sadness and all-sufficing strength. Yet the peace is not the dreadful peace of death; it is the peace that passeth understanding."

FOUR VIEWS of the Lincoln plaster mask by Clark Mills now in the Lincoln Museum, Washington, D. C. Photographed by Lloyd Ostendorf and reproduced by courtesy of Colonel R. B. Truett and Stanley W. McClure.

233

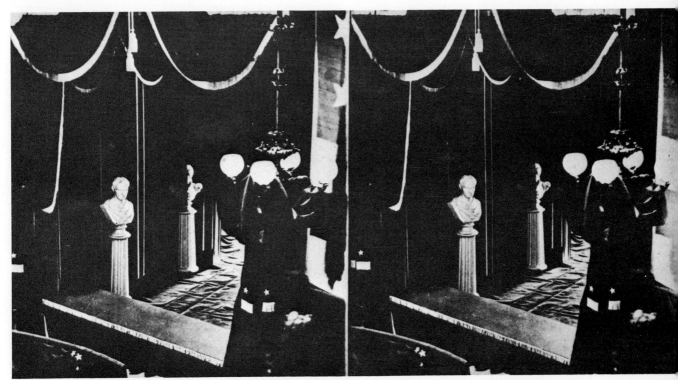

Chicago Historical Soc

AN UNPUBLISHED STEREOGRAPH by Jeremiah Gurney, Jr., of the mourning draperies in the Governor's Room of the New York City Hall, where Lincoln's body lay in state. On the left is a bust of Daniel Webster; on the right, of Andrew Jackson.

"I SAW HIM IN HIS COFFIN," wrote David R. Locke, an author whom the President admired. "The face was the same as in life. Death had not changed the kindly countenance in any line. There was upon it the same sad look that it had worn always, though not so intensely sad as it had been in life. It was as if the spirit had come back to the poor clay, reshaped the wonderfully sweet face, and given it an expression of gladness. . . . It was the look of a worn man suddenly relieved."

234

Springfield State Historical Library   O–119

THE LAST PHOTOGRAPH FROM THE FLESH, a multiple-lens photograph by Jeremiah Gurney, Jr., City Hall Governor's Room, New York, Monday, April 24, 1865.

THE PRESIDENT LIES IN STATE, flanked by Admiral Charles H. Davis (left) and General Edward D. Townsend. The cameraman, Jeremiah Gurney, Jr., took two exposures, one with a multiple-lens camera. As soon as Secretary of War Stanton heard of the photographs, he ordered their destruction. General John A. Dix reported that he had confiscated and destroyed the larger negative and the sole print from it. He sent Stanton a print from the four-lens plate, with a request that the negative be spared. Stanton at once issued orders to destroy the remaining plate and all the prints. The sole print sent to him by General Dix was preserved by Stanton and was given by his son to John G. Nicolay. It remained forgotten until 1952 when Ronald Rietveld, a fifteen-year-old student, discovered it among the Nicolay papers in the Illinois State Historical Library.

235

Original sketch owned by Charles Hamilton

THE LAST PORTRAIT.   As Lincoln lay in his coffin in the New York City Hall, artist Pierre Morand made this pencil sketch of the tired face at rest. Published here for the first time, it is the last-known portrait of Lincoln from the flesh.

A French-American businessman and artist, Morand had met the wartime President in Washington. "In life Mr. Lincoln's features and movements impressed me so vividly," he later observed, "that I made several good sketches of him in various attitudes in June, 1864." Morand made this final hurried portrait at 2:00 A.M. on the morning of April 25, 1865.

CROWDS OF MOURNERS filing past the coffin in the New York City Hall were portrayed in this illustration (at left) entitled "Citizens Viewing the Body at City Hall," which was published in *Harper's Weekly*, May 6, 1865. So vast was the throng that even during the night and early morning viewers were allowed only a few moments to glance into the coffin before they were hurried on by the guards. Perhaps Morand was permitted to stand with the pallbearers for the few minutes needed to make the sketch above.

236

VIGNETTE PORTRAIT, 1864,
Norton and Luther, Cleveland, Ohio

RARE STANDING PORTRAIT

THE MAN WHO SHOT LINCOLN. Three unpublished photographs of handsome and eccentric Booth, a distinguished actor who was a Southern sympathizer. In 1863, Booth had performed before the President in a play called *The Marble Heart*, but the role he chose for the night of April 14, 1865, was far more dramatic. To a desk clerk at the Washington National Hotel, he grimly predicted "some fine acting tonight" at Ford's Theatre. Arming himself with a pocket pistol and a dagger, he quietly entered the side door of the theatre and made his way to the President's box. For a moment he eyed him through a tiny hole in the door. Then he entered, fired a ball into the back of Lincoln's head, and leaped to the stage. He escaped on horseback, but twelve days later he was cornered in a Virginia barn and mortally wounded.

On May 6, 1865, *Harper's Weekly* carried advertisements offering photographs of Lincoln at ten cents and photographs of Booth at twenty-five cents.

VIGNETTE PORTRAIT by Fredricks, New York

A SINGLE SOLDIER STANDS GUARD over the empty theatre in which Lincoln was killed. This and the next photograph, both taken the day after the murder, were recently presented to the Illinois State Historical Library by Gideon Stanton, grandson of Lincoln's Secretary of War. Previously unpublished.

THE PRESIDENT'S BOX IN FORD'S THEATRE. An unpublished photograph of the place where Lincoln spent his last conscious moments. The assassin caught his spur in the draped flag (right) as he leaped eleven feet to the stage. Booth's left leg was broken, hampering his flight.

THE COFFIN AND FUNERAL CARRIAGE at Indianapolis. Lincoln's body was returned to Springfield by almost the same route the President-elect had taken to Washington. At every stop crowds thronged to see the remains of the man they now called "the Savior of the Union." First publication from a rare photograph in the Lincoln National Life Foundation.

THE HEARSE which carried Lincoln's body home. Surmounted by black plumes, this sable-shrouded carriage bore the President from Chicago to Springfield where, on May 3 and May 4, his face was looked upon for the last time by his old friends and neighbors. Courtesy Chicago Historical Society.

Courtesy Lincoln Memorial University, Harrowgate, Tennessee

LINCOLN'S HOME IS DRAPED IN BLACK.   Like other homes in the nation, Lincoln's own residence in Springfield was draped with a display of sorrow. This rare carte-de-visite view, probably taken from a window across the street, shows a seldom-photographed side of his home at Eighth and Jackson streets. A group of Springfield youngsters posed quietly while a local photographer, F. W. Ingmire, took this picture.

APOTHEOSIS PICTURES OF LINCOLN. The crack of Booth's derringer made a martyr and a legend of Abraham Lincoln. On these two pages are ten carte-de-visite views, composites of paintings and photographs which helped to turn Lincoln into an American folk-hero. Scarcely a parlor album in the North was without at least one such maudlin memento.

Original photographs of Lincoln were used in the making of these popular examples of American folk-art.

Lincoln Memorial University

THE FOUNDER AND THE PRESERVER OF THE UNION.
Apotheosis.
Entered according to Act of Congress by Thurston, Herline & Co., in the year 1865, in the Clerk's Office of the District Court of the Eastern District of Pennsylvania.

APOTHEOSIS OF WASHINGTON & LINCOLN.

Entered, according to Act of Congress, in the year 1865, by J. A. Arthur, in the Clerk's Office of the District Court for the Eastern District of Pennsylvania.
WASHINGTON & LINCOLN (APOTHEOSIS.)
S. J. Ferris, Del. Photo. and Pub. by Phil. Pho. Co., 722 Chestnut St.

Ostendorf collection

"$5.00-bill pose"   O–92

Engraved   O–91

Engraved, with mourning border   O–91

O–55

O–91

O–91

PRINTS of the oversized "Columbia's grief"
were originally sold in the street by a one-armed Civil War veteran.

O–36

THE NOMINEE IS CASUAL.   At fifty-one, in November, 1860, Lincoln appears relaxed but alert before the camera.

244

O–82

As is the President. Three years later, at fifty-four, he seems wary and tough, but just as casual.

Reverse photograph O–1   O–118

A YOUNG MAN BECOMES AN OLD MAN in less than twenty years. Between the first and last pictures of Lincoln there is a contrast so startling that the portraits seem of different men. The vigorous man of thirty-seven looks younger than his years. And the weary fifty-six-year-old President seems at least a decade older. The first picture was taken by N. H. Shepherd in 1846, the last by Alexander Gardner on April 10, 1865. Only a single original was made of each photograph.

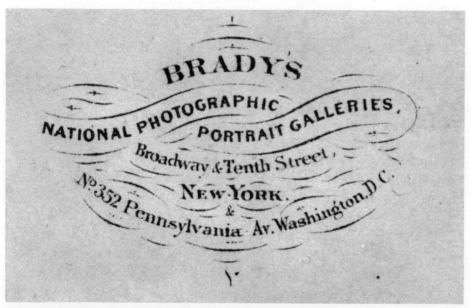

A GALLERY OF SIGNED PHOTOGRAPHS. Imprint and signature of Lincoln from the back of a Brady photograph signed in 1862 for his friend, Representative Thomas Dawes Eliot. Courtesy Eliot's granddaughter, Mrs. Clara R. Frothingham.

"IS THIS ALL YOUR FRIEND WANTS?" wrote Lincoln on the back of a signed photograph. "It seems very little to ask."

Today this rare signed photograph is worth more than Lincoln's weekly salary as President.

Apparently Lincoln never refused to put his signature to a camera portrait, but not many of his photograph-collecting contemporaries were farsighted enough to ask. Even the soldiers who visited him were content with the unsigned photographs he personally gave away, apparently not deeming his autograph of much importance.

From time to time signed pictures of Lincoln turn up—a choice example was recently bought by a poor Negro woman at a church bazaar for only one dollar—but most of those which now make their appearance for the first time are forgeries. During the compilation of this volume the authors examined many alleged signed photographs of the Civil War President, some of which were obvious fabrications.

Forgeries may easily be identified not only because the ink and signature differ from Lincoln's but because most forgers blunder in the selection of a photograph on which to place their handicraft. Instead of using an original portrait bearing the camera artist's name on the back, such as Lincoln invariably gave away, they often fabricate his signature on a cheap reprint which may lack even the name or trademark of a photographer.

Illinois State Historical Library O–14

OF GREAT RARITY are signed beardless photographs of Lincoln. This handsome example, nine inches in height, bears the same inscription as the portraits on the next page. The original was sent by Lincoln with a covering letter dated November 2, 1860, to dry-goods salesman George F. Smith, of Plantsville, Connecticut.

Chicago Historical Society O–14

SIGNED BEARDLESS PORTRAITS

O–21

PRESENTED BY Lincoln to Benjamin
F. Prescott at Exeter, New Hampshire, and now owned by Prescott's
son.

O–2

SOLD AT the Oliver R. Barrett auc-
tion in 1952 for $550 and now in
the collection of Dr. Paul B. Free-
land of Nashville, Tennessee.

Meserve collection O–28

The J. B. Speed Memorial Museum, Louisville, Ky.   O-55

THE MOST FAMOUS SIGNED PHOTOGRAPH.   The longest inscription ever penned
by Lincoln on a photograph was to the mother of his old friend, Joshua Fry
Speed: "For Mrs. Lucy G. Speed, from whose pious hand I accepted the present of an Oxford Bible twenty years ago. Washington, D. C., October 3, 1861.
A. Lincoln."

Lincoln National Life Foundation Lincoln National Life Foundation Copy in Ostendorf collection
O–71 A O–71 B O–71 B

THREE SIGNED AT ONE SITTING

THE LEFT PAIR WAS SENT BY LINCOLN to Mrs. Henry P. Westerman of Pekin,
Illinois. The cover, bearing the free franking signature of the President's secretary, John Hay, is postmarked October 11, 1864. The photograph at the right,
probably signed at the same time, is from a copy print in the Ostendorf collection, the original of which has disappeared.

BOTH OF THESE CARTE-DE-VISITE PHOTOGRAPHS bear the imprint of Brady's Washington studio. Lincoln's favorite portrait of himself (left) bears an exceptionally bold signature. When white space was available, Lincoln signed on the glossy paper of the photograph, rather than on the cardboard mount.

Ostendorf collection   O–87 C

Collection of Elsie O. and Philip D. Sang
O–90 B

A PAIR OF SIGNED VIGNETTES

253

A. Lincoln & Son.

254

A. LINCOLN, & SON

ONLY TWO PHOTOGRAPHS were signed by Lincoln with this unusual inscription. Both were presented to Gustave E. Matile, undersecretary to John Hay. Three months after Lincoln's death,

Lincoln National Life Foundation   O–93

Matile presented the handsome example (opposite) to his friend, Charles M. Gormly, whose grandson, Stephen G. Schwartz, provided the copy negative for reproduction in this volume. The second photograph (above, left), identical except for the ruled oval border, was given by Matile to the Kellogg Public Library in Green Bay, Wisconsin. An exact copy of a signed photograph of the pose (above, right) is in the Lincoln National Life Foundation.

RETOUCHED PHOTOGRAPHS
PHOTOGRAPHS OF ENGRAVINGS
COMPOSITES OF PHOTOGRAPHS

A GALLERY OF EARLY LIKENESSES originally sold as authentic photographs. In Lincoln's era it was an accepted practice to retouch or alter photographs or to sell composite pictures as original poses. All photographers did it. Their purpose was not to deceive but to provide "photographs" which would meet the public demand for interesting or unusual scenes and portraits.

Meserve collection   (M–101)   Variant O–2

A LIKENESS BASED ON HESLER'S PHOTOGRAPH is Thomas Doney's mezzotint, first published in 1860. On July 30, 1860, Lincoln wrote to Doney and thanked him for a copy of "the picture (I know not the artistic designation)." Meserve considered it a second pose from the Hesler sitting of 1857 (M–101).

257

Lincoln National Life Foundation O–2   Ostendorf collection Variant O–2

A TRUE PHOTOGRAPH AND A RETOUCHED COPY.   On February 28, 1857, Alexander Hesler took the famous photograph of Lincoln (left) in Chicago. About seven months earlier, so went the story, Lincoln had posed for William H. Masters of Princeton, Illinois. No photograph by Masters has turned up, and there is no evidence that he took Lincoln's picture. But the Masters Studio, avoiding the use of the word *photograph*, widely distributed the picture (right) "from the Masters Portrait made July 4, 1856, at Princeton, Ill." So extensive were the sales of the Masters portrait, a reversed and retouched copy of Hesler's likeness, that it has become the best known of Lincoln faked photographs.

AN UNUSUAL COMPOSITE PHOTOGRAPH (right) made up from two authentic Hesler portraits. The face is taken from the 1857 Hesler photograph (left) and the hair from the 1860 Hesler photograph (center).

Hesler 1857 photograph (M–6) O–2

Hesler 1860 photograph (M–27) O–29

Composite fake photograph (M–18)

LINCOLN GETS HIS HAIR COMBED

Illinois State Historical Library O–9   Ostendorf collection   Variant O–9

BEARDLESS Lincoln in 1858   BEARD ADDED early in 1861

LINCOLN GETS FALSE WHISKERS

WHEN LINCOLN TOOK OFFICE as the first bearded President, people wanted pictures of him with whiskers. Several photographers and artists met this demand simply by painting beards on earlier photographs.

Ostendorf collection   O–33

Courtesy Mrs. H. S. Ritter, Quincy, Ill.
Variant O–33

THE CLEAN-SHAVEN LINCOLN OF 1860 WITH A FALSE BEARD.   Above (left) is an authentic photograph of Lincoln taken in Springfield in 1860. At right is the same portrait with whiskers artistically supplied.

Ostendorf collection   O–2

Ostendorf collection   Variant O–2

AN IMMACULATE BEARD WAS ADDED by artist-publisher Doney to his famous engraving (right) based on the Hesler 1857 photograph (left).

BRASS CAMPAIGN-ALBUM LOCKET (actual size). Copies from paintings or photographs, these small tintypes, or ferrotypes, were made into tokens, medals, buttons, and badges which promoted Lincoln's election.

THE TINTYPE AT RIGHT, much enlarged from the original, is an extremely rare portrait apparently based on a campaign lithograph of 1860. According to an earlier owner it was found in Lincoln's law-office desk.

Ostendorf collection

TINTYPES HELPED LINCOLN TO BECOME PRESIDENT. Miniatures from prints or retouched photographs were widely distributed during his two campaigns.

Ostendorf collection   Variant O–17   Ostendorf collection   Variant O–14

1860 CAMPAIGN TINTYPES

TWO MINIATURE TINTYPES (much enlarged) set into circular brass frames and buttons. On the verso of each is a portrait of the vice-presidential candidate, Hannibal Hamlin. The beardless 1860 Brady photograph (left), with face reversed, was extremely popular. The beardless 1858 portrait by Cole (right) was also a favorite with Lincoln supporters.

1864 CAMPAIGN TOKENS

Left: REVERSED VARIANT tintype button (O–86) from the U. I. Harris collection in St. Louis, Missouri; *center:* Reversed variant tintype pin (O–91), Ostendorf collection; *right:* Variant paper photograph (O–91) mounted in brass, Ostendorf collection. All enlarged from the miniature originals.

One photograph becomes two. A copy of T. Painter Pearson's 1858 ambrotype of Lincoln (right), taken in Macomb, Illinois. The variants (below) led Meserve to conclude that Pearson took at least two pictures of Lincoln at this sitting. A carte-de-visite variant of Pearson's ambrotype is in the Lincoln Museum in Washington, D. C.

Ostendorf collection   O–8

Meserve collection   (M–10)   Variant O–8

Meserve collection   (M–11)   Variant O–8

Meserve collection
Photograph detail (M–47)   O–65

Meserve collection
Painted variant (M–48)

McClellan is taller and more dramatic in the artist's painting (right) of the historic conference with Lincoln at Antietam. On the left is a detail of the original photograph by Gardner which served the artist as a model. McClellan's outstretched hand (at right) seems to point to the illegible signature of the artist on the left edge of the painting. The painted version was given a number (M–48) in the Meserve enumeration of Lincoln photographs.

Ostendorf collection   O–76

TO IMPROVE THE PHOTOGRAPH by Gardner (left), John G. Nicolay hired an artist to paint in a background of the Executive Mansion furnishings, even including Andrew Jackson's portrait on the wall and John Bright's photograph on the mantel. The carpet, which looked worn in the original picture, was transformed into a luxurious Oriental rug. The artist tried to straighten Nicolay's right leg, but it looks more deformed in the "corrected" version. When Nicolay went to Paris shortly after Lincoln's death, he allowed Paris photographer E. Talons to issue cartes-de-visite of this version.

Ostendorf collection   Variant O–76

266

Ostendorf collection O–91

ORIGINAL PHOTOGRAPH by Anthony Berger on February 9, 1864.

(M–87) Variant O–91

A VARIANT by Brady's retoucher, an artist named Bersch, who "polished" the original photograph.

Meserve collection
(M–108) Variant O–91

LINCOLN'S FACE is softer and handsomer in this second retouched variant.

Ostendorf collection
Variant O–91

A THIRD VARIANT was issued by the Brady gallery as a vignette carte-de-visite.

A PARENT PHOTOGRAPH AND THREE OFFSPRING

BRADY TOOK THE PICTURES—artists "improved" them. *Left:* Original carte-de-visite photograph by Brady, January 8, 1864. *Right:* Head detail from Brady photograph (left), considered a separate pose by Meserve. *Below left:* Copy direct from the original by Anthony Berger, February 9, 1864. Lincoln and Tad are looking at an album of Brady photographs. *Below right:* An artistic revision of the original photograph (left), issued by Anthony Berger in 1865 after he opened his own gallery in New York. Berger redesigned the chair and dressed up the album to make it look like a family Bible. The changes were probably made to evade Brady's copyright.

Ostendorf collection   (M–75)   O–84

Meserve collection   (M–107)   Variant O

Ostendorf collection   O–93

Ostendorf collection   Variant O–93

268

One of the most popular of Lincoln photographs was the Brady portrait of Lincoln and Tad. Many variations were issued in the form of retouched photographs, paintings, lithographs, and woodcuts. Some were published as photographs. Three variations were numbered by Meserve as separate poses, two of which (M–40 and M–41) are illustrated on this page.

A composite oval engraving issued by Currier and Ives. "President Lincoln at Home reading Scriptures to his Wife and Son." Meserve numbered it M–41.

Meserve collection   (M–41)   Variant O–93

Meserve collection   (M–40)   Variant O–93

An artistic background added to the original Brady photograph. Meserve numbered it M–40.

PRESIDENT LINCOLN & FAMILY.

Ostendorf collection   Variant O–93

A carte-de-visite photograph of an engraving, presumably based on an 1866 painting by Carpenter. This composite work is one of the most common of all Lincoln pictures.

Meserve collection (M–19) Variant O–17

A NEW BEARD, A NEW BODY
An early composite Lincoln

THE FAMOUS COOPER UNION PORTRAIT by Brady is shown (above, left) in a
waist-deep variant, identified by Meserve as a separate pose. On the right is the
same photograph, reversed and with a beard. But Lincoln's face has now been
grafted on the body of Henry Clay, and the Civil War President, much shrunk,
stands proudly against the background of the original Clay engraving. This
"photograph" was widely circulated during Lincoln's lifetime. In 1856 the
same body of Clay had carried the head of Presidential candidate John C.
Frémont.

National Archives O-86   Carl Haverlin collection, New York   Carl Haverlin collection, New York

LINCOLN HOLDS A DOCUMENT put in his hands by the artist who created the classic poses on the right. Using the head of Lincoln from the photograph by Brady taken January 8, 1864 (left), the artist gave Lincoln (center and right) a new body, a Grecian setting, and a manuscript to hold. These two rare prints from a larger artistic work were published in 1864 as carte-de-visite photographs by Jno. Holyland, a Washington photographer.

Lincoln National Life Foundation collection
Variant head O–91

Lincoln National Life Foundation collection
Variant head O–84

ASSUMING Alexander Hamilton's body, Lincoln leans authoritatively on the Constitution. The head of Andrew Jackson was also engraved on this body.

LINCOLN's big head rests awkwardly on the narrow shoulders of Martin Van Buren. This body was also used to accommodate the head of Francis P. Blair, Jr.

Lincoln National Life Foundation collection
Variant head O–95

Lincoln National Life Foundation collection
Variant head O–92

LIKE James Buchanan, his inept predecessor, Lincoln stands with easy grace in an atmosphere of dignity. This body probably served originally as that of Martin Van Buren.

WITH the body of John C. Calhoun, Lincoln expands his chest with pride as he clutches Washington's cape.

FOUR NEW BODIES FOR LINCOLN.   Even while Lincoln was alive, enterprising artists created composite engravings of him, using his head mounted on the bodies of other men to save effort and costs in new art work and plates. Some of these composite engravings were copied by the camera and sold as photographs.

A PHOTOGRAPHIC COPY of artist John Henry Brown's miniature of Lincoln. Union soldier Henry H. Ladd, of the 24th Michigan Volunteers, wrote "Father Abraham" on his album copy.

A PHOTOGRAPHIC COPY of a lithograph shows Lincoln with wavy hair. This rare French carte-de-visite was sold by E. Nuerdein in 1863 at his Paris gallery.

PHOTOGRAPHIC COPY of a lithograph published by Gibson & Co. in southern Ohio, 1865.

THE ORIGINAL of this carte-de-visite was a large decorative steel engraving based on Brady's famous five-dollar bill photograph (O–92).

PHOTOGRAPHIC FAKES.   These engravings and lithographs, made to resemble camera portraits, were copied and widely circulated as carte-de-visite photographs.

All photographs Ostendorf collection

A CARTE-DE-VISITE PHOTOGRAPH (1865) of an artist's conception of the Lincoln family, originally printed as a lithograph. Robert T. Lincoln stands behind his father, Tad is at the President's side, and Mrs. Lincoln appears on the right. The child at Mrs. Lincoln's feet has never been identified.

Left: THIS TRANQUIL but improbable domestic scene appeared as a cabinet photograph after Lincoln's death. Perhaps based on a painting, it shows Mrs. Lincoln in an unaccustomed pose of affection and Tad, who hated books, pouring eagerly over a volume. Robert looks on with justifiable concern. *Right:* A photograph of William Sartain's engraving of 1866. Lincoln's pose is based on the photograph (O–91) taken by Berger at Brady's gallery on February 9, 1864, an original which inspired many artists. Willie's picture is on the wall, and Robert, wearing a moustache, bears a startling resemblance to John Wilkes Booth!

PHOTOGRAPHIC FAKES OF THE LINCOLN FAMILY. Composite engravings or lithographs which were published and sold as photographs.

274

Ostendorf collection   Ostendorf collection

Left: CARTE-DE-VISITE of President Lincoln and his cabinet, photographed from a larger engraving in 1862. *Right:* A group of mounted Brady studio portraits with fancy borders reproduced in miniature on a carte-de-visite photograph, 1864.

Ostendorf collection

Ostendorf collection

Left: SOJOURNER TRUTH, noted evangelist, presents Lincoln with a Bible in this unusual composite photograph. The figure of Lincoln was added by the artist. *Right:* "Lincoln and generals in Council before Richmond" is the title of this photograph of a lithograph. In 1865 it was distributed as an authentic photograph for carte-de-visite albums.

MORE "MADE-UP" PHOTOGRAPHS

Ostendorf collection O-41

LINCOLN AS THE CAMERA SAW HIM.   First publication direct from an original print. An extremely rare oval photograph showing the entire, unretouched pose exactly as recorded by the camera of C. S. German. In the Illinois State Historical Library are two original prints of this 1861 portrait.

Courtesy Judge Carl E. Wahlstrom
Variant O-41

National Archives (M-34) Variant O-41

ANOTHER version of German's handsome photograph is this reversed tintype variant, a copy of which was personally presented by Lincoln in 1861 to Private Jerome W. Bell of the 11th Vermont Volunteers.

. . . AS THE ARTISTS SAW HIM. Goggle-eyed and well fed is Lincoln (above) after his face was worked over by an artist. This often published variant shows an almost vapid President. The print in the National Archives is from the Herbert Wells Fay retouched cabinet-size negative which the owner valued at $10,000.

Meserve collection   Variant O-41

PUBLISHED in 1894 by Herbert Wells Fay as the "McNulty-Butler Lincoln," this vignette portrait is merely another retouched version of the C. S. German 1861 photograph.

A REVERSED, retouched tintype of German's photograph, preserved in its original case.

Lincoln National Life Foundation, Fort Wayne   Variant O-41

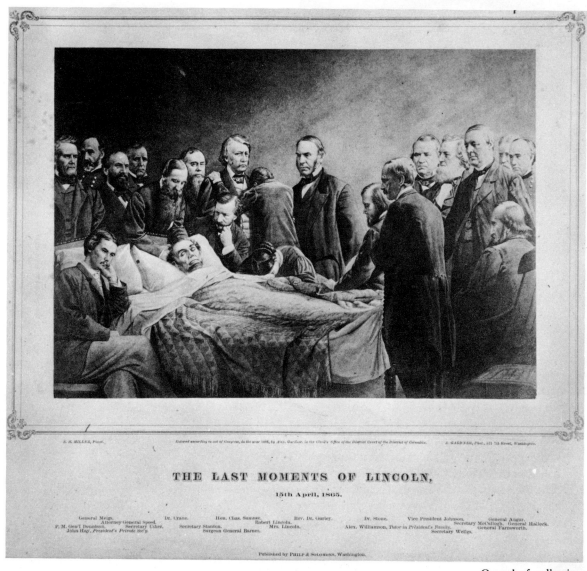

THE LAST MOMENTS OF LINCOLN,

15th April, 1865.

General Meigs.   Dr. Crane.   Hon. Chas. Sumner.   Rev. Dr. Gurley.   Dr. Stone.   Vice President Johnson.   General Augur.
Attorney General Speed.   Robert Lincoln.   Secretary McCulloch. General Halleck.
P. M. Gen'l Dennison.   Secretary Usher.   Secretary Stanton.   Mrs. Lincoln.   Alex. Williamson, *Tutor in President's Family*. General Farnsworth.
John Hay, *President's Private Sec'y.*   Surgeon General Barnes.   Secretary Welles.

Published by PHILP & SOLOMONS, Washington.

Ostendorf collection

FOR THIS COMPOSITE SCENE, Alexander Gardner used many authentic photographs from his gallery, but an artist added Lincoln's head. Originally a mounted photograph, it was published by Philp & Solomons, Washington, D. C., from the Gardner negative, and was copyrighted on September 22, 1866. This is believed to be the first book publication.

CARTE-DE-VISITE COPY of a drawing reproduced by photography for parlor albums.

tendorf collection

"DEATH-BED OF LINCOLN" was painted by John H. Littlefield, once a law student in Lincoln's office. The artist used photographs as models for the twenty-five people gathered in the death room, but his profile of the dying Lincoln shows a first-hand acquaintance. Copyrighted in 1866 by Littlefield, the scene was published in photographic enlargements (11¼ inches by 18¼ inches) by Washington photographer John Goldin.

Death-Bed of Lincoln.

PHOTO-CARTOONS

O-55   Ostendorf collection   Variant head O-55

THE PHOTO-CARTOONS OF THE CIVIL WAR ERA were first drawn or painted, after which a retouched photograph of Lincoln's head was mounted on the caricature body. The cartoon was then recopied by a camera and issued as a carte-de-visite photograph.

Most often used by artists was the 1861 photograph of Lincoln (above, left), issued by many firms in New York and Philadelphia and readily available to cartoonists. At right is one of the most popular carte-de-visite cartoons, entitled, "I Wish I Was in Dixie." Like the cartoons on the next page, it has a photo-head based on the 1861 portrait.

Meserve collection

Meserve collection

Ostendorf collection

Ostendorf collection

Above, left: ANOTHER VERSION of "I Wish I Was in Dixie." *Above, right:* A most interesting cartoon on the 1864 election, "The Winning Hand," picturing Lincoln and McClellan in a card game. *Below, left:* A conscription cartoon, showing "Granny" Lincoln spoon-feeding the draft to the people. *Below, right:* Another conscription cartoon, showing the President administering "A Bitter Draught" of "Dr. Lincoln's ready relief pills," consisting of cannon balls.

Meserve collection (M–100) O–118   Ostendorf collection (M–94) Variant O–118

AN ORIGINAL PHOTOGRAPH . . . AND A REFINED COPY. The original enlargement (left) by Alexander Gardner from the cracked collodion plate is the last
picture taken of Lincoln. On the right is the revamped portrait, a product of
the Gardner gallery, with Lincoln's face retouched and softened. Removal of
the contrasting tones makes his face almost vacuous. This altered likeness, re-
garded by Meserve (M–94) as a separate pose, was published in 1865 as a
vignette carte-de-visite by Philp & Solomons of Washington, D. C.

SCARCELY A YEAR goes by without the discovery and publication of a "new" Lincoln photograph. Usually it is a photograph of some tall black-bearded man wearing a stovepipe hat and standing in a crowd. And, nearly always, the picture turns out to be that of some other man who from a distance looks like the Civil War President.

In this section appear the most widely publicized of the doubtful photographs, plus a few which are definitely spurious or fabricated.

Courtesy C. C. Tisler, Ottawa, Ill.

SAID TO BE A PHOTOGRAPH OF LINCOLN AND DOUGLAS at the time of the debates, this picture was taken in front of the old Eames house at 117 East Lafayette Street, Ottawa, Illinois. The tall central figure by the pillar was believed to be Lincoln and the short man to the left was thought to be Douglas.

Supposedly taken on August 21, 1858, the original photograph was first published in the Ottawa *Daily Republican-Times* of August 21, 1941, at which time it was owned by L. B. Olmstead of Somonauk. While it is possible that Lincoln and Douglas are in the picture, no positive identification can be made since the original photograph has disappeared.

THE PEORIA STAR FEB. 13, 1938

RANDOLPH HOTEL 1858 A. LINCOLN 1858

Photo taken on one of Lincoln's visits to Macomb, showing a number of Macomb residents of that day and Lincoln atop the historic old hotel. Because the original of this picture was becoming worn with age, it recently was copied for preservation purposes. The accompanying story tells of the occasion upon which this photo was taken.

THE TALL FIGURE ON THE ROOF, second from the right, is supposed to be Lincoln posing on the roof of the Randolph Hotel at Macomb, Illinois, with a group of ladies. Presumably taken on October 26, 1858, the day after Lincoln made a speech in Macomb, this interesting old photograph was first published in *The Peoria Star*, February 13, 1938.

The story goes that after lunch Lincoln, who had posed for Painter Pearson at his gallery two months earlier, agreed to let the photographer take his picture with some ladies who were serving on a political committee. Unfortunately, only the newspaper reproduction of this photograph is available and no identification is possible without an examination of the lost original print.

Ostendorf collection

Two "Lincolns" appear in this hirsute gathering.   The bearded man at
the far end of the right side of the picnic table was said to be Lincoln, but his
face is too youthful for that of the President. The man in the left foreground
also bears a striking resemblance to Lincoln, but a close examination shows
many differences in their features. The original of this interesting picture is a
stereograph, of which only one half is shown here.

FIRST PUBLISHED by Frederick Hill Meserve as a questionable photograph of Lincoln in his *Supplement Number Four*, privately printed in New York, 1955. Meserve gave it a "B" designation instead of a number.

Lincoln National Life Foundation, Meserve "B"

THE TALL FIGURE bears a great resemblance to Lincoln. Identified as "A. Lincoln" in pencil on the front of the original stereograph, of which only one half is shown here, the man in the stovepipe hat could easily be another person. Originally owned by Charles F. Thomas, who supervised the building of the Capitol dome in 1861, this rare view is now in the collection of the Lincoln National Life Foundation.

GUARDING THE EXECUTIVE MANSION at the outbreak of the Civil War is the battalion organized by Major General Cassius M. Clay. According to some authorities, Lincoln posed with the assembled troops, here shown at the rear of the White House on April 29, 1861. This photograph was first published in *Old Cane Springs, a Story of the War between the States in Madison County, Kentucky* (1937) by Dr. Jonathan Truman Dorris.

MAJOR GENERAL CASSIUS M. CLAY (right) resigned his commission as commanding officer of the "Washington Clay Guards" in 1863 to accept the post of Minister to Russia.

Enlarged detail from photograph of the "Washington Clay Guards"

THE TALL MAN WEARING THE STOVEPIPE HAT was identified as President Lincoln by Meserve (M–125, *Supplement Number Four*), but in this enlargement he appears to have a white beard! It was also claimed that Mrs. Lincoln is looking out of the second-story window, third from left. There is no evidence that either the President or the First Lady appears in this picture.

National Archives

STANDING WITH THIS GROUP OF INDIANS is a tall, bearded man with a plug hat who closely resembles Lincoln. He is in the center of the picture, under the left arch, just behind the plume of an Indian. Although the dress suggests a period earlier than the 1860's, the bearded personage looks more like Lincoln than the figure in the previous photograph. No one has yet claimed that Lincoln appears in this interesting scene, but the photograph is reproduced here to illustrate how easy it is to find a "new Lincoln" in any group picture in which the faces are not clearly visible.

Head detail O–93

LINCOLN AND TAD

Ostendorf collection

THE FACE OF LINCOLN in the "shawl" portrait was evidently based on the famous photograph of Lincoln and Tad looking at a Brady album (O–93). No history of the "shawl" picture has come to light and no unretouched print has turned up— additional evidences that it was fabricated.

"THE ONLY PHOTOGRAPH OF LINCOLN WEARING A SHAWL" is what Meserve called this spurious photograph (M–126) in his *Supplement Number Four*. First published as an illustration in Doc Aubery's *Recollections of a Newsboy in the Army of the Potomac, 1861–65*, the portrait then revealed far less detail than in this retouched version. In his book Aubery relates how, as a boy, he gave a newspaper to Lincoln, then watched him read it. No doubt some imaginative artist created this portrait to dramatize Aubery's story, embodying in it the apparel so often associated with the Civil War President—the stovepipe hat, the steel-rimmed spectacles, the shawl, and the big boots.

THE HANOVER JUNCTION "LINCOLN."   A tall, bearded man in a top hat stands at the right of the train. From a distance he looks very much like Lincoln, who, on November 18, 1863, passed through Hanover Junction en route to Gettysburg. In 1952 this view received widespread publicity as a newly discovered photograph of Lincoln. Later research showed that the President arrived in Hanover Junction too late in the day for a cameraman to take his picture.

National Archives

UNRETOUCHED ENLARGEMENT OF HANOVER JUNCTION "LINCOLN." The nose of the bearded man is too sharp, his body too heavy, his beard too thin to be Lincoln's. Even his necktie is unlike those worn by the Civil War President.

"ABRAHAM LINCOLN AND SON" was the identification given to this old daguerreotype (right) by the owner who sent it to the Lincoln National Life Foundation. The boy slightly resembles Tad, but close examination reveals that the features of the man are very different from those of Lincoln.

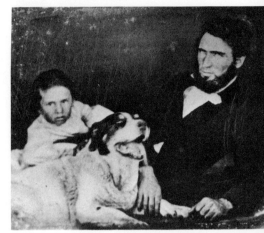

Courtesy Lincoln National Life Foun▪

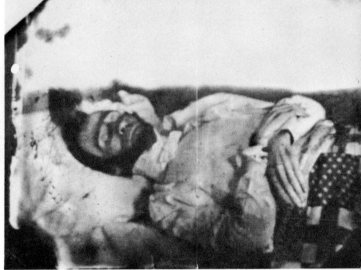

Courtesy Lincoln National Life Foun▪

Left: IDENTIFIED AS "remains of Abraham Lincoln / the Greatest Man of Our Century," this alleged photograph, actually a drawing made about 1865, was published by George Koch of Indianapolis, Indiana. *Right:* "Is this Lincoln?" was the title of an article about this photograph which appeared in *The Saturday Evening Post* on February 15, 1941. The answer is *no*. The beard is too heavy on the sides of the face, the style of clothing was long out of date in 1865, and Lincoln wore a dark tie in death. Even as early as the 1840's it was customary to take pictures of the dead, for the subject presented no problem of motion and could be photographed under poor lighting conditions by a longer exposure.

THE LINCOLN FAMILY

"I DON'T KNOW WHO MY GRANDFATHER WAS," said Lincoln. "I am much more concerned to know what his grandson will be."

Despite Lincoln's jest, the people from whom he came and those with whom he lived intimately are of great interest to us, for many of them helped to change his life. In this gallery of faces familiar to Lincoln are his family and close friends, his law partners, and even his political enemies—all those who knew him or touched him.

There is no photograph of Lincoln's mother, Nancy Hanks, who died at the age of thirty-four in 1818, more than twenty years before the invention of the camera. Herndon wrote that she was "above the ordinary height in stature, weighed about 130 pounds, was slenderly built, and had much the appearance of one inclined to consumption. Her skin was dark; hair dark brown; eyes gray and small; forehead prominent, face sharp and angular, with a marked expression of melancholy which fixed itself in the memory of everyone who ever saw or knew her." And Lincoln declared that she was "highly intellectual by nature, had a strong memory, acute judgment, and was cool and heroic."

A year after the death of Nancy Hanks, Lincoln's father, Thomas, married Sarah Bush, a remarkable woman who loved and aided the future President. Lincoln said of this woman, whom he called "my angel mother": "She has been my best friend in this world." Sarah Bush outlived her famous stepson by four years. When interviewed after Lincoln's murder, she said, weeping: "I did not want Abe to run for President, and I did not want to see him elected. I was afraid that something would happen to him, and when he came down to see me, after he was elected President, I still felt, and my heart told me, that something would befall Abe, and that I should never see him again."

THE MOST IMPORTANT SINGLE INFLUENCE in the life of Lincoln, Sarah Bush Johnston was a widow for three years before she married Thomas Lincoln on December 2, 1819. With her three children she moved into the rude Indiana cabin built by her new husband. A woman of dignity and kindness, she encouraged her stepson in his youthful studies.

This only surviving photograph of Sarah Bush, taken about 1865 when she was seventy-seven, was once owned by her granddaughter, Mrs. Harriet Chapman of Charleston, Illinois.

ACCORDING TO HIS FAMOUS SON, Thomas Lincoln was "a wandering laboring-boy" who "grew up literally without education." A carpenter by trade and barely able to write his name, he spent much of his life in a restless quest for a profitable farm. He endowed the future President with a powerful physique, a love of storytelling, and a knowledge of pioneer woodcraft.

The reflected light on the shirt indicates that this photograph is probably a copy of an old daguerreotype. It was purchased by Lieutenant O. V. Flora during the Civil War from a member of the Lincoln family. Under the picture is written in an early hand: "Thomas Lincoln, Born 1778, Died 1851." Many scholars doubt its authenticity, but the rugged, angular features of the subject, so dramatically Lincolnesque, match contemporary descriptions of Thomas Lincoln.

Illinois State Historical Library

Courtesy Lincoln Memorial University, Harrogate, Tenn.

SARAH BUSH LINCOLN
(stepmother)

THOMAS LINCOLN, A TRADITIONAL PORTRAIT
(father)

DAGUERREOTYPE by N. H. Shepherd, Springfield, Illinois, 1846.

AGE forty-two. Photograph by an unknown artist, Springfield, about 1860.

AGE forty-three. Photograph by Brady, Washington, D. C., 1861.

AGE forty-three. Photograph by Brady, Washington, D. C., 1861.

HIS WIFE
MARY TODD LINCOLN

Ostendorf collection

THE FIRST LADY IN HER INAUGURAL GOWN.   This attractive photograph was taken by Mathew B. Brady at his Washington, D. C., studio in 1861. Mrs. Lincoln loved flowers and often posed with them in her hair or hands.

Courtesy Burton N. Gates and Judge Carl E. Wahlstrom

Mrs. Lincoln with a group of Indians who had come to Washington to visit the President. The First Lady stands at the extreme right, and in the rear center is Lincoln's private secretary, John G. Nicolay. For comparison, Mrs. Lincoln and John G. Nicolay are shown (opposite) in similar poses. A previously unpublished stereograph (right half) taken by Brady in 1862.

John G. Nicolay
Photo by Brady, Washington, D. C.

Mrs. Lincoln, in bonnet
Photo by Preston Butler, Springfield, 1861

Ostendorf collection

Ostendorf colle

Ostendorf collection

coln National Life Foundation

Meserve collection

Left: MRS. LINCOLN IN MOURNING ATTIRE after Willie Lincoln's death in 1862. *Center:* Mrs. Lincoln early in 1862. *Right:* Mrs. Lincoln, about 1863.

◄ THE SUNLIGHT POURING THROUGH THE GLASS ROOF of the White House Conservatory has created a pattern of light and dark which emphasizes the youth of the girls and the age of Mrs. Lincoln in the stereograph on the opposite page. In one print of this stereograph, John G. Nicolay identified himself, but did not mention the First Lady.

The short man on the extreme left has been mistakenly identified as Vice-President Andrew Johnson, to whom he bears a very slight resemblance. The tall figure next to him was once thought to be Lincoln, but his short neck, heavy body, wide-bridged nose, long upper lip, and small ears show very little similarity to those of the Civil War President.

Ostendorf collection   Meserve collection

Top left: ROBERT TODD LINCOLN in Springfield, 1860. The earliest-known photograph, previously unpublished. *Top right:* Robert Todd in 1861, Springfield, Illinois. *Bottom left:* First publication of a photograph by J. Goldin, Washington, D. C., about 1865, the original of which was once owned by Lincoln's friend, Judge David Davis. *Lower right:* Robert Todd in Washington, about 1864.

Illinois State Historical Library   National Archives

ROBERT TODD LINCOLN

His oldest son, born August 1, 1843; died July 26, 1926, age eighty-three.

Illinois State Historical Library

Illinois State Historical Library

Ostendorf collection

Ostendorf collection

ROBERT TODD LINCOLN

Top left: ROBERT TODD LINCOLN in November, 1861. From a carte-de-visite by an unknown photographer. First book publication. *Top right:* Robert Todd when a student at Harvard, probably early in 1861. First book publication. *Lower left:* Robert Todd with a dapper moustache, Washington, D. C., 1865, possibly taken by J. Goldin. *Lower right:* Another pose, Washington, D. C., possibly by J. Goldin.

Top left: WILLIE LINCOLN about 1855, from an ambrotype taken in Springfield. The earliest-known photograph. *Top right:* Willie in Springfield in 1860. *Lower left:* Willie (standing) and Tad Lincoln pose with Mrs. Lincoln's nephew, Lockwood Todd, at Brady's gallery in 1861. *Lower right:* Willie, taken by Brady, Washington, D. C., 1861.

WILLIE LINCOLN

WILLIAM WALLACE ("Willie"), born December 21, 1850; died of acute malarial infection, February 20, 1862, age eleven. The favorite of his father, Willie was actually Lincoln's third son (Edward Baker Lincoln died in 1850 at the age of four and no photograph of him is known.) Willie strikingly resembled Lincoln in mind and body and was described by Mrs. Lincoln's cousin as "a noble and beautiful boy . . . frank and loving."

Ostendorf collection   Chicago Historical Society

Top left: TAD LINCOLN as a baby, ambrotype taken in Springfield in 1855 or 1856. *Top right:* Tad poses for Brady in 1861, age eight. *Lower left:* Mrs. Lincoln with her sons Willie (left) and Tad (right), taken in Springfield late in 1860 by Preston Butler and reproduced as an engraving on the cover of *Frank Leslie's Illustrated News*, December 15, 1860. *Lower right:* Tad in Washington, 1862, from a signed carte-de-visite photograph in the Ostorn H. Oldroyd collection of the Lincoln Museum.

Illinois State Historical Library   Lincoln Museum, Washington, D. C.

TAD LINCOLN

Thomas ("Tad"), born April 4, 1853; died July 18, 1871, age eighteen.

"TAD was a merry, warm-blooded, kindly little boy, perfectly lawless," wrote Lincoln's secretary, John Hay. "He ran continually in and out of his father's cabinet [room] interrupting his gravest labors and conversations with his bright, rapid speech—for he had an impediment which made his articulation almost unintelligible. . . . He would perch upon his father's knee, and sometimes even on his shoulder, while the most weighty conferences were going on . . . dropping to sleep at last on the floor when the President would pick him up and carry him tenderly to bed."

Ostendorf collection

TAD LINCOLN in a soldier's uniform, a rare vignette photograph, previously unpublished.

Ostendorf collection

National Archives

Left: TAD as a Zouave (1861) holding a miniature rifle at port arms. Tad presented a carte-de-visite of this photograph to his neighborhood friend, Julia Taft. *Right:* Tad poses for Brady in 1865.

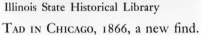

TAD IN CHICAGO, 1866, a new find.   HIS FATHER IN CHICAGO, 1859.

TAD AND HIS FATHER.   Similar poses for Chicago photographer Sam M. Fassett. Both father and son look earnest and alert in these portraits, which reveal the great difference in their features. The picture of Tad, previously unpublished, was discovered late in 1960 by Lloyd Ostendorf among the piles of old photographs recently acquired by the Illinois State Historical Library from the heirs of Lincoln's associate, Judge David Davis.

Meserve collection

ROBERT TODD LINCOLN
First son of Lincoln (August 1, 1843–
July 26, 1926), died at eighty-three. He
was the last direct descendant with the
surname of Lincoln.

Chicago Historical Society

THOMAS ("TAD") LINCOLN
Fourth son (April 4, 1853–July 15, 1871),
died at eighteen.

THE LAST OF THE LINCOLNS
Sons who survived him

◄ A UNIQUE FOUR-IMAGE PLATE OF TAD from the National Archives collection in Washington. The images are inverted stereographs, and when the right and left views of either horizontal pair are transposed, the two pictures may be viewed in three dimensions through a stereoscope. There were once many such four-image photographs of Lincoln, but all were cut apart many years ago.

Ostendorf collection
ROBERT TODD AS A YOUNG LAWYER

Illinois State Historical Library
LINCOLN'S DAUGHTER-IN-LAW

HIS SON, ROBERT TODD LINCOLN, became a noted statesman. The long and distinguished career of Robert Todd Lincoln began when, after leaving Harvard, he served brilliantly as captain on the staff of General Grant during the closing months of the Civil War. His wife, Mary Harlan Lincoln (1847–1937), weighed only eighty-nine pounds at the time of her marriage. The President called her "Little Mary." When she was being courted by Robert, she and her betrothed often rode by carriage with Mr. and Mrs. Lincoln to a mill in Virginia where they bought freshly ground meal. She was about thirty when the photograph (above, right) was taken.

Ostendorf collection

Ostendorf collection

MINISTER TO GREAT BRITAIN

IN OLD AGE, ABOUT 1922

AN ASTUTE ATTORNEY, Robert Todd Lincoln was appointed secretary of war in Garfield's cabinet (1881) and after Garfield's murder was the only cabinet member retained by Chester A. Arthur.

He declined to be a candidate for the Presidency and in 1889 accepted the post of minister to Great Britain. His last active years were spent as president of the Pullman Company (1897–1911).

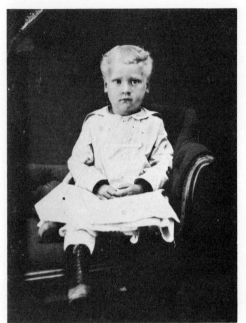

Ostendorf collection   Lincoln National Life Foundation   Illinois State Historical Lib

ABRAHAM ("JACK") LINCOLN II

(August 14, 1873–March 5, 1890) was the second child of Robert T. Lincoln. He was born eight years after the President's murder and died at the age of seventeen. *Left:* At age four, a tintype presented by Robert T. Lincoln to the Lincoln's former maid, Mariah Vance. *Center:* At age five, in 1878. First book publication of a carte-de-visite photograph by H. Rocher of Chicago. *Right:* At about eleven, in 1884.

Lincoln National Life Foundation

JESSIE LINCOLN at two and one-half years, photographed by H. Rocher in 1878. The third child of Robert Todd Lincoln, Jessie was born in 1875 and died in 1948.

MARY LINCOLN at age nine. Daughter of Robert Todd Lincoln and Mary Harlan Lincoln, she was born in 1869 and died in 1938. This photograph was taken in 1878 by H. Rocher of Chicago.

Lincoln National Life Foundation

Lincoln National Life Foundation

Left: MARY LINCOLN with her only child, Lincoln Isham. Granddaughter of the President, Mary Lincoln married Charles Isham in 1891.

Below: JESSIE LINCOLN and her daughter, Mary. Jessie married Warren Beckwith in 1897.

Ostendorf collec

Below: MARY LINCOLN BECKWITH (at left), the great-granddaughter of Lincoln, was born in 1898 and is unmarried. LINCOLN ISHAM (center), great-grandson of the President, was born in 1892. He is married to Leahalma Correa but has no children. ROBERT LINCOLN BECKWITH (right), another great-grandson, was born in 1904. He is married to Hazel Holland Wilson but also has no children. With the deaths of childless Lincoln Isham and Robert Lincoln Beckwith and unmarried Mary Lincoln Beckwith, the direct line of descent from Abraham Lincoln will come to an end.

Ostendorf collection

Ostendorf collection

Ostendorf colle

LINCOLN'S RELATIVES
CLOSE FRIENDS
AND ASSOCIATES

COUSINS OF LINCOLN'S MOTHER, John and Dennis Hanks were close to Lincoln in his youth and later told many tales about him. John, a genial but illiterate frontiersman, split rails with the future President and in 1831 journeyed with him to New Orleans on a flatboat. During the 1860 Decatur Republican party convention, John Hanks and Isaac Jennings created a sensation by carrying into the convention hall a pro-Lincoln sign supported by two fence rails split by Lincoln on the Macon County farm. Dennis, who lived to be ninety-three, remembered many episodes in Lincoln's boyhood, some of which he probably exaggerated. Once he claimed that he had saved seven-year-old Abe's life by pulling him out of the treacherous waters of Knob Creek.

Ostendorf collection

DENNIS HANKS

Ostendorf collection

JOHN HANKS

He lived with the Lincoln family in Indiana from about 1823 to 1827.

Ostendorf collection

DENNIS HANKS

A dignified pose in a stovepipe hat which Dennis probably borrowed from the photographer. His rugged face has many Lincoln characteristics.

316

endorf collection   Ostendorf collection

Left: STANDING BESIDE THE OLD LINCOLN HOME are Lincoln's second cousins, Dennis and John Hanks (with beard). Dennis married Lincoln's stepsister, Elizabeth. *Right:* Another view, with John on the left. Published here for the first time in a book. Both photographs were taken in 1865 by J. L. Campbell.

LINCOLN HELPED TO BUILD THIS OLD CABIN.   From April, 1830, to July, 1831, the future President lived in this rude one-room cabin in Macon County, about ten miles west of Decatur, Illinois. The logs were cut by John Hanks, and years later Dennis recalled: "Abe helped put up a cabin fur Tom on the Sangamon, clear fifteen acres fur carn an' split walnut rails to fence it in. . . . We lived jest like the Indians, 'cept we talked religion and politics."

Tintype in Ostendorf collection

SHE LIVED IN THE SAME CABIN WITH LINCOLN.   Elizabeth Johnston Hanks, stepsister of the President, was one of the eight persons crowded into the tiny one-room cabin in which Lincoln spent much of his youth. This rare, previously unpublished tintype, taken about 1858, was inspired by the gift of a dress from Lincoln. "The outfit and bonnet in the picture," explained the daughter of Dennis and Elizabeth Hanks in 1901, "once belonged to Aunt Mary Lincoln, and Uncle Abe gave it to my mother as a gift when he came on one of his visits to our home in Charleston [Illinois]. My mother had to let out the hems as she was taller than Aunt Mary. My father thought her pretty much a grand lady when she put this outfit on, and he told her he wished she'd 'go down and have her picture took in it.' "

Courtesy Adin Baber,
Hanks family authority

LINCOLN'S UNCLE HOLDS AN OLD CAPLOCK RIFLE. Posing stiffly with his old rifle is Fielding Hanks (1783–1861), brother of Lincoln's mother. Hanks died on August 13, 1861, soon after the start of the Civil War, and was buried at Compton, Kentucky.

A COUSIN FROM VIRGINIA. Abigail Lincoln (1801–82) was the first cousin of the President's father, Thomas Lincoln. She married Joseph Coffman of Dayton, Virginia.

Courtesy John W. Wayland, author of
The Lincolns in Virginia

"COUSIN JOHN" OWNED THE LINCOLN HOME. Standing at the door of the log cabin built in Goosenest Prairie, Illinois, by Lincoln and his father is John J. Hall, believed to be a second cousin of Lincoln. Hall lived in the cabin with the Lincolns

Library of Congress

between 1829 and 1831, and by right of long occupancy was its owner on July 23, 1891, when Root of Chicago took this picture. On January 31, 1861, President-elect Lincoln visited Hall here for the last time and observed, "Oh, my God, John! Once the old cabin, now the White House!"

HE THREATENED TO SHOOT HIS COUSIN ABE. When Yankee soldiers under General Sheridan burned his barn in 1864, John Lincoln (1824–89) expressed a keen desire to put a bullet through his second cousin, Abraham Lincoln. John owned a farm near the homesite of "Virginia John" Lincoln, great-grandfather of the President. This photograph of John and the pictures of Lincoln's Virginia cousins (below) are reproduced by courtesy of John W. Wayland, author of *The Lincolns in Virginia*.

VIRGINIA COUSINS WITH A FAMILY RESEMBLANCE

Left to right: JACOB NICHOLAS LINCOLN (1821–80) of Lacey Springs, Virginia, son of Thomas Lincoln's first cousin, David Lincoln. MARY ELIZABETH LINCOLN PENNYBACKER (1827–1905), daughter of Thomas Lincoln's first cousin, Colonel Abraham Lincoln, had the President's nose and eyes. ABRAHAM "A. B." LINCOLN (1822–1905), of Lacey Springs, Virginia, son of David Lincoln, is said to have served as a militia captain in the Civil War. He had Lincoln's eyes. BENJAMIN FRANKLIN LINCOLN (1813–64), son of David Lincoln, was a cavalryman in the 10th Virginia Cavalry and was known as "Uncle Frank" Lincoln.

Illinois State Historical Library

MRS. NINIAN W. EDWARDS (Elizabeth P. Todd), sister of Mary Todd Lincoln, holds her grandson, Edward Lewis Baker II. From an ambrotype taken in 1859.

Illinois State Historical Library

NINIAN WIRT EDWARDS, brother-in-law of Lincoln and son of Governor Ninian Edwards, was prominent in Springfield society and politics. Lincoln was married in his home, November 4, 1842.

Illinois State Historical Library

MRS. NINIAN W. EDWARDS, age forty, from a daguerreotype taken about 1853.

Illinois State Historical Library

THE EDWARDS BOYS, Albert S. and Charles, cousins of the Lincoln boys. In this miniature daguerreotype Charles (right) shows a striking resemblance to Tad Lincoln.

Ostendorf collection   Illinois State Historical Library

SPRINGFIELD IN-LAWS

Upper left: MRS. WILLIAM SMITH WALLACE (Frances Todd), sister of Mary Todd Lincoln. From a tintype taken about 1858. *Upper right:* DR. WILLIAM SMITH WALLACE, Lincoln's brother-in-law, a Springfield druggist, received a commission as a brigadier general from Lincoln. *Lower left:* MRS. CLARK MOULTON SMITH (Ann Maria Todd), sister of Mary Todd Lincoln, bore a close resemblance to Lincoln's wife. *Lower right:* CLARK MOULTON SMITH, Lincoln's brother-in-law, a merchant at whose store the Lincolns traded.

Illinois State Historical Library   Illinois State Historical Library

Illinois State Historical Library

Illinois State Historical Library

Upper left: DR. JOHN TODD, uncle of Mary Todd Lincoln, a physician who was described by a friend as "suave and diplomatic, calm, quiet, and affable." *Upper right:* ELIZABETH TODD GRIMSLEY (1825–95), daughter of Dr. Todd and cousin of Mrs. Lincoln. From a photograph taken in 1861 by J. A. Kennan of Philadelphia while Mrs. Grimsley was en route to the White House, where she spent six months. *Lower left:* MAJOR JOHN TODD STUART (1807–85), a cousin of Mary Todd Lincoln, encouraged Lincoln to study law, served with him in the Illinois legislature at Vandalia in 1832, and was his law partner from 1837 to 1841. From a family album photograph taken in 1860 and published here for the first time. *Lower right:* MARY NASH STUART, wife of Major Stuart, from a photograph in a Lincoln family album.

Illinois State Historical Library

Illinois State Historical Library

William H. Townsend collection   Ostendorf collection   William H. Townsend collecti

LINCOLN'S SISTERS-IN-LAW

Left: MARTHA K. TODD, half-sister of Mrs. Lincoln and wife of Confederate Major Clement C. White of Selma, Alabama. A visitor at the White House, she deceived her brother-in-law, President Lincoln, by taking supplies to the South. *Center:* ELODIE ("DEDEE") TODD, half-sister of Mrs. Lincoln and wife of Confederate Colonel N. H. R. Dawson of Selma, Alabama. She visited the Lincolns in Springfield and was later a White House guest. *Right:* EMILIE TODD ("Little Sister"), half-sister of Mrs. Lincoln and wife of Confederate General Ben Hardin Helm. She spent six months at the Lincoln home in Springfield in 1855. She visited the White House in 1861 and again in 1863 after her husband was killed in action.

Ostendorf collection

From a painting owned by
William H. Townsend, Lexington, Ky.

Left: Mrs. Charles H. Kellogg (Margaret Todd), half-sister of Mary Todd Lincoln, lived in Cincinnati. Photograph taken in 1860. *Right:* Robert Smith Todd, father-in-law of Lincoln, from a portrait painted about 1836. Todd lived in Lexington, Kentucky, but visited the Lincolns in Springfield several times. They named their eldest son after him.

Other in-laws of Lincoln include Levi O. Todd, brother of Mary Todd Lincoln, of whom no photograph is available.

Ostendorf collection

Ostendorf collection

Ostendorf collection

J. Winston Coleman, Jr.

LINCOLN'S REBEL BROTHERS-IN-LAW

Top left: CAPTAIN DAVID H. TODD, half-brother of Mrs. Lincoln, fought with the Rebel Army and died in 1863 of wounds received at Vicksburg. *Top right:* ALEXANDER H. TODD, half-brother of Mrs. Lincoln, fought in the Confederate Army and was killed at Baton Rouge in 1863. *Bottom left:* GENERAL BEN HARDIN HELM, husband of Mrs. Lincoln's half-sister, Emilie, was a graduate of West Point. He refused Lincoln's offer of a commission, joined the Rebel Army, and was killed at Chickamauga in 1863. *Bottom right:* DR. GEORGE R. C. TODD, youngest brother of Mrs. Lincoln, a Confederate surgeon in the Civil War. Intelligent but temperamental, he treated Union prisoners brutally and was called "the most degraded of all the rebels." No photograph was available of SAMUEL TODD, another half-brother of Mrs. Lincoln, who fought with the Confederate Army and was killed at Shiloh in April, 1862.

THE MINISTERS IN LINCOLN'S LIFE.
Lincoln never joined any church. In
his youth, he came very close to athe-
ism, declaring later that he had been
"tossed amid a sea of questionings."
Eventually he accepted the tenets of
Jesus Christ as "settled and fixed moral
precepts," and he compared his reli-
gious code with that of an old man he
once knew. "When I do good I feel
good, and when I do bad I feel bad, and
that's my religion."

Bloomington Historical Society

REVEREND PETER CARTWRIGHT, circuit-
riding Methodist preacher and politician,
was defeated by Lincoln for Congress in
1846. In this old daguerreotype he has
parked his spectacles on his head!

Illinois State Historical Library

Illinois State Historical Library

Left: REVEREND CHARLES DRESSER was an Episcopalian priest who performed the
marriage ceremony for Lincoln and Mary Todd on Friday, November 4, 1842, then
in 1844 sold Lincoln his home at Eighth and Jackson streets in Springfield. *Right:*
REVEREND JAMES SMITH, pastor of the First Presbyterian Church in Springfield,
preached the services at Eddie Lincoln's funeral in 1850. Lincoln attended his church
with Mrs. Lincoln, who was a member, but when asked to join said that he "couldn't
quite see it."

Lincoln Memorial University
collection

Illinois State Historical
Library

Ostendorf collectio

DOCTOR FRIENDS—IN ILLINOIS

Left: DR. JOHN ALLEN, physician to Lincoln, organized the first temperance society in New Salem and practiced medicine there between 1831 and 1839. *Center:* DR. ANSON G. HENRY attended the Lincoln family in Springfield and was a guest at the White House. *Right:* DR. AMOS WILLARD FRENCH (and wife). Dr. French was Lincoln's dentist in Springfield. First publication from a rare original ambrotype taken November, 1861.

Lincoln National Life   National Library of Medicine   Ostendorf collection
Foundation

DOCTOR FRIENDS—IN WASHINGTON

Left: DR. EUGENE ALEX HOUSTON identified himself on the back of an old carte-de-visite photograph as "Pill maker and Plaster spreader to Old Abe." First publication. *Center:* DR. ROBERT KING STONE, Lincoln's White House physician, described the President as "the purest-hearted man with whom I ever came in contact." *Right:* DR. CHARLES A. LEALE was the first doctor to reach Lincoln's side after he was shot at Ford's Theatre. He worked all night to aid the dying President and held his hand when he died the next morning at the Peterson house.

Lincoln Memorial
University collection

Ostendorf collection

BOYHOOD FRIENDS—KENTUCKY

Left: SAMUEL HAYCRAFT, historian of Elizabethtown, Kentucky, was an old friend of the Lincoln family. He employed Lincoln's father as a carpenter to help build a mill and mill race. In 1860 he corresponded with Lincoln about the candidate's family and youth. *Right:* AUSTIN GOLLAHER (1805–98) was a boyhood playmate of Lincoln, who fished and caught wild ducks with the future President. In the autumn of 1816 he saved young Abe from drowning in Knob Creek. Most of Lincoln's early friends and associates passed their youth long before the camera was invented in 1839 and were photographed (if at all) in old age. This picture of the venerable Austin Gollaher is from a rare tintype formerly owned by the Gollaher family.

Ostendorf collection

Ostendorf collection

BOYHOOD FRIENDS—INDIANA

Left: REVEREND ALLEN BROONER AND HIS WIFE. Brooner and Lincoln were close friends as boys. Their mothers died only a week apart from the "milk sick" and were buried in the same plot. The two youths once walked more than fifty miles to Vincennes to buy a hunting rifle in partnership for $15.00. When Lincoln moved to Illinois in 1830, he sold his interest in the gun to Brooner. *Right:* JOHN WESLEY HALL AND HIS WIFE. An intimate friend of young Lincoln, "Wes" Hall, the son of a local tanner, often stayed overnight at the Lincoln cabin, sleeping in the loft with young Abe. He recalled that one night Tom Lincoln, who was illiterate, asked his son to read aloud. Abe regaled them with passages from Franklin's *Autobiography*.

330

Ostendorf collection   Ostendorf collection   Ostendorf collection

Left: JOSEPH GENTRY, a companion of Lincoln in his youth, helped make the coffin in which Nancy Hanks was buried. *Center:* JAMES GENTRY, owner of Gentry's store, hired young Lincoln in 1828 to go with his son, Allen, on a flatboat carrying produce to New Orleans. *Right:* DAVID TURNHAM AND HIS WIFE. Six years older than Lincoln, Turnham (1803–84) went to the same school and lent Lincoln the first law book he ever studied, *The Revised Statutes of Indiana.*

Ostendorf collection

Above: JOSIAH "OLD BLUE NOSE" CRAWFORD AND HIS WIFE. Crawford employed Lincoln as a farm hand, and Abe once pulled corn for fodder for three days in Crawford's field to pay for a copy of Ramsay's *Life of Washington* which he had borrowed and damaged. When the hired hand confided his Presidential aspirations to Mrs. Crawford, she laughed: "You'd make a purty President, with all your tricks and jokes, now wouldn't you?" And Lincoln answered, "Oh, I'll study and get ready, and then the chance will come." *Right:* JAMES GRISBY was a member of the socially prominent Grisby family. His brother, Aaron, married Lincoln's sister, Sarah.

Ostendorf collection

331

CLOSE FRIENDS FROM NEW SALEM

Ostendorf collection   Ostendorf collection

Left: MARY ANN RUTLEDGE was the mother of Lincoln's legendary sweetheart, Ann Rutledge. She and her husband, James Rutledge, ran the New Salem Inn, a rude tavern at which Lincoln boarded for several months. Lincoln and Ann Rutledge studied grammar together, and he may have courted her. *Right:* MARY OWENS was a buxom, blue-eyed maid, a year older than Lincoln, to whom the future President proposed in 1837. After she rejected him, the chagrined suitor consoled himself with the thought that "her skin was too full of fat" and she had a "weather-beaten appearance." Years later Mary Owens explained that "Mr. Lincoln was deficient in those little links which make up the chain of a woman's happiness—at least it was so in my case."

Ostendorf collection   Ostendorf collection   Ostendorf collection

LINCOLN LODGED AT THEIR HOMES

Left: WILLIAM BUTLER, a New Salem friend, invited Lincoln to live with him as long as he wished. *Center:* DANIEL GREEN BURNER was a clerk in the Berry and Lincoln store in New Salem. Lincoln lodged for some months at the home of his father, Isaac Burner. *Right:* REVEREND JOHN M. CAMRON, a millwright and a Presbyterian minister, was the co-founder with James Rutledge of New Salem. Lincoln boarded at Camron's house when he first came to New Salem in 1831.

Ostendorf collection   Ostendorf collection

Left: WILLIAM G. GREENE, JR., known as "Slicky Bill," was hired as an assistant to Lincoln in Denton Offutt's store and at the New Salem mill. Both slept at the store in a bed so narrow that when one turned over, "the other had to do likewise." They remained lifelong friends, and during the war Lincoln appointed Greene a collector of internal revenue at Peoria. *Right:* JOSHUA A. MILLER was a New Salem blacksmith at whose forge Lincoln spent much of his leisure time. For a brief period before turning to the law, Lincoln planned to become a smith.

Ostendorf collection   Ostendorf collection

Left: JAMES SHORT was a farmer who aided Lincoln during the three-year period when the future lawyer was working as a surveyor. At the lowest ebb in Lincoln's fortunes, his creditors sued and levied on his personal property, including his surveying instruments. "Uncle Jimmy" Short bid the instruments in when they were sold on execution and gave them back to Lincoln. *Right:* NANCY POTTER GREEN was the wife of local justice of the peace, Squire Bowling Green, at whose home Lincoln was a constant visitor. When Lincoln began to study law in 1834, he argued his first cases (without pay) before Squire Bowling Green. Legend has it that Nancy Potter Green nursed Lincoln back to sanity after Ann Rutledge's sudden death in 1835.

Illinois State Historical Library   Lincoln Memorial   New Salem Museum
University

LINCOLN WAS CLOSE TO THE ARMSTRONGS

Left: JACK ARMSTRONG, leader of the gang of rowdies known as the "Clary's Grove boys" challenged Lincoln to a wrestling match and became his fast friend when the fiercely contested bout ended in a draw. From an unpublished daguerreotype owned by Henry Holland of New Holland, Illinois. *Center:* HANNAH ARMSTRONG, Jack's wife, patched Lincoln's shirts while he rocked her baby's cradle or played with the older children. When Lincoln received two buckskins as pay for a survey, Hannah "foxed" his pants with the skins to protect him from briars. *Right:* WILLIAM D. ARMSTRONG ("Duff"), Hannah's son, was defended by Lincoln in 1858 when tried for murder. Lincoln negated the testimony of an alleged eyewitness by proving from an old almanac that there was no moonlight on the night of the murder. This rare photo shows Duff as a Union soldier in 1861.

Tintype in Illinois State   Illinois State Historical Library   Illinois State Historical
Historical Library   Library

MORE NEW SALEM FRIENDS

Left: MENTOR GRAHAM, a schoolmaster, tutored Lincoln and aided him in his studies. Graham persuaded Lincoln to study surveying, later said that he was the "most studious . . . in the pursuit of knowledge and literature . . . among the 5,000 I have taught in schools." *Center:* JOHN CALHOUN, surveyor for Sangamon County, took Lincoln on as a deputy surveyor. When Calhoun's wife jested about the deputy's appearance, Calhoun retorted, "For all that, he is no common man!" *Right:* ISAAC ONSTOT, son of a New Salem cooper, studied grammar and arithmetic with Lincoln by the light of the burning shavings in his father's cooper shop. Portrait from an ambrotype, about 1856.

Illinois State Historical Library   Illinois State Historical Library

SPRINGFIELD PROFESSIONAL FRIENDS

Left: ROBERT IRWIN, Lincoln's banker, ran a general store in Springfield and sold Lincoln nearly $2,000 worth of goods in a ten-year period. While Lincoln was President, Irwin handled his bank account and paid his taxes and bills in Springfield. *Right:* ROLAND WEAVER DILLER, Lincoln's druggist, recalled that "Mr. Lincoln used to drop in and sit for hours with friends and neighbors around the drug store stove, swapping stories and discussing public questions."

Courtesy Isaac Hilliard and the Speed Museum, Farmington

LINCOLN'S MOST INTIMATE FRIEND—a rare, unpublished daguerreotype. No man ever got closer to Lincoln than Joshua Fry Speed, a wealthy Springfield merchant, portrayed here with his beautiful wife Fanny Henning Speed and her little sister, Maria Louisa Henning. When Lincoln rode into Springfield on April 15, 1837, carrying all his property in his saddlebags, he went to A. Y. Ellis & Co. to buy bedding on credit. Ellis' partner and clerk, Joshua Speed, invited him to share a double bed above the store. Soon the two men were exchanging secrets; and when Speed married Fanny Henning early in 1842, Lincoln soon followed his example with Mary Todd.

This original daguerreotype of 1853 shows that Joshua F. Speed grew a beard seven years before Lincoln. Mary Louisa Henning (left), youthful sister of Mrs. Speed (center), later married J. J. B. Hilliard. Her son, Isaac Hilliard, is now the owner of the daguerreotype from which Lloyd Ostendorf made this copy.

Illinois State Historical Library   Illinois State Historical Library   Illinois State Historical Library

SPRINGFIELD FRIENDS

Left: OZIAS M. HATCH, a close personal friend, traveled with Lincoln to Iowa in 1859 and to Antietam in 1862. He frequently advised the President on political issues relating to Illinois. *Center:* RICHARD OGLESBY, a lawyer and firm supporter of Lincoln, promoted the scheme to have John Hanks carry the fence rails into the Decatur convention hall in 1860. Pictured here in an 1850 daguerreotype, Oglesby subsequently became a major general in the Union Army and the governor of Illinois. *Right:* OWEN LOVEJOY, a congressman from Illinois, was a valued friend of the wartime President. He hated slavery and used his home at Princeton as a station for the Underground Railway before the war.

Illinois State Historical
Library

Ostendorf collection

"TO THIS PLACE, and the kindness of these people, I owe everything," said Lincoln in his last speech to his Springfield friends. *Extreme left:* JESSE K. DuBOIS first met Lincoln in the Illinois state legislature, later backed him as a dark horse in the 1860 Presidential campaign. *Left:* JOHN E. ROLL, who helped Lincoln build the flatboat on which he journeyed to New Orleans in 1831, was an intimate friend and neighbor in Springfield. His sons played with the Lincoln boys.

338

Illinois State Historical Library

SPRINGFIELD FRIENDS

Top left: JUDGE DAVID DAVIS. An unpublished daguerreotype (1854) of the saga-cious 300-pound jurist who traveled the circuit with Lincoln. Davis was the chief strategist in Lincoln's nomination for President and was appointed to the Supreme Court in 1862. *Top right:* MRS. DAVID DAVIS was a warm friend of Lincoln and often entertained him in her home at Bloomington. *Bottom left:* LYMAN TRUMBULL, a jurist of great distinction, served with Lincoln in the Illinois Legislature in 1840, later opposed him for United States senator. He was three times elected to the Sen-ate. *Bottom right:* JULIA JAYNE TRUMBULL was, before her marriage to Lyman Trumbull, a close friend of Mary Todd and a bridesmaid at her wedding to Lincoln. When the political rivalry between their husbands became intense, the friendship ended.

339

LINCOLN'S LAW PARTNERS

DURING his long career as an attorney, Lincoln had three law partners who influenced his life. John Todd Stuart served in the Black Hawk War and in the Illinois state legislature with Lincoln. A cousin of Mary Todd, he persuaded Lincoln to study law, lent him his lawbooks, and then made him his partner (April 12, 1837–May 14, 1841).

Illinois State Historical Library
JOHN TODD STUART

Left: STEPHEN TRIGG LOGAN, Lincoln's second law partner (1841–44), was an astute judge and one of the most brilliant attorneys in Illinois. He helped his youthful partner develop a keen legal mind. *Right:* MRS. STEPHEN T. LOGAN, from a carte-de-visite photograph by C. S. German.

Illinois State Historical Library

Illinois State Historical Library

LINCOLN'S THIRD AND LAST law partner was William Henry Herndon (right), who was nine years Lincoln's junior. From 1844 until the day Lincoln died, Herndon was a loyal and trusted associate, submerging his own ambitions to advance the reputation of his partner. Although undistinguished as an attorney, Herndon later wrote one of the most interesting and valuable biographies of Lincoln. This picture was taken about 1870.

Ostendorf collection
WILLIAM H. HERNDON

Lincoln Memorial University collection

NOT ACTUALLY A PARTNER but a close associate of Lincoln was huge Ward Hill Lamon (above), the burly, boisterous prosecuting attorney of Danville. Lincoln trusted him completely. He appointed Lamon his personal bodyguard and marshal of the District of Columbia. Lamon was away on a special mission when Lincoln was shot. This rare, early photograph shows Lamon at the period when he was intimate with Lincoln. Mrs. Ward Hill Lamon, from a carte photograph. First book publication.

341

Illinois State Historical Library

HIS LAWYER FRIENDS

Top left: ORVILLE H. BROWNING was an intimate friend of Lincoln who traveled from Springfield to Washington, D. C., with the President-elect. In 1861 he was appointed senator from Illinois to complete Stephen A. Douglas' term. *Top center:* EDWARD D. BAKER, a very close friend after whom Lincoln named his second son, introduced Lincoln at his first inaugural. Appointed a brigadier general at the outbreak of war, he was killed in 1861 at Ball's Bluff. *Top right:* NORMAN B. JUDD made the speech placing Lincoln's name in nomination at the 1860 convention and accompanied him to Washington in 1861. *Bottom left:* T. LYLE DICKEY joined the Republican party when it was first organized in Illinois and later broke away from it. Lincoln said that "he did not know of any of his friends he felt so badly about losing as Dickey." *Bottom center:* HENRY C. WHITNEY, a close associate of Lincoln in the circuit days (1854–60), wrote *Life on the Circuit with Lincoln* (1892). *Bottom right:* LEONARD SWETT traveled the circuit with Lincoln and helped to groom him for the Presidency. In his youth he resembled Lincoln.

MORE LAWYER FRIENDS

Left: ALBERT T. BLEDSOE, an Episcopalian minister and graduate of West Point, occupied an office next to Lincoln while practicing law in Springfield (1839–47). Bledsoe later served in the Confederacy as assistant secretary of war. *Center:* JUDGE JOSEPH GILLESPIE fought in the Black Hawk War and was admitted to the bar in 1836. While serving in the Twelfth General Assembly, he came to admire Lincoln's amazing memory and legal ability. This photograph is from a daguerreotype taken in 1845. *Right:* SAMUEL H. TREAT, judge on the Illinois Supreme Court and presiding judge of the Eighth Judicial Circuit, owned one of the largest private libraries in Illinois. He introduced Lincoln to *Joe Miller's Jest Book*, from which the future President drew many of his humorous tales.

YOUTHFUL LAWYERS WHO STUDIED WITH LINCOLN

Left: COLONEL ELMER E. ELLSWORTH was the colorful leader of the New York Zouaves and the first Union officer killed in the Civil War. Lincoln wrote a classic letter of condolence to Ellsworth's parents and held his funeral in the White House. *Center:* HENRY B. RANKIN is the author of *Personal Recollections of Abraham Lincoln*. His claim that he served with Lincoln as a law student is disputed by some scholars. *Right:* GIBSON W. HARRIS was the first student to study law with Lincoln and Herndon (1845) and was a frequent visitor at the Lincoln home.

Lincoln National Life Foundation

Ostendorf collection

Courtesy W. O. Stoddard, Jr.

Courtesy Wayne C. Temple

LINCOLN'S WHITE HOUSE SECRETARIES

Top left: JOHN G. NICOLAY, inventor and newsman, was appointed Lincoln's private secretary in 1860. This portrait, from a rare ambrotype taken in 1859, is published here for the first time. *Top right:* JOHN HAY was a law student who came to Washington at Nicolay's request and joined him as assistant private secretary. Hay was later a distinguished poet and United States secretary of state, collaborating with Nicolay in a classic ten-volume biography of Lincoln (1890). This photograph is from a damaged plate taken by Brady in 1861. *Bottom left:* WILLIAM O. STODDARD, originally authorized only to sign land patents for Lincoln, was promoted to a desk in Hay's office. He often carried Presidential messages, which he called "paper latch-keys, opening every door." *Bottom right:* NOAH BROOKS was a White House correspondent and close friend of Lincoln who often accompanied him on trips. He later wrote a biography of the President.

Illinois State Historical Library

Ostendorf collection

Courtesy Dr. John E. Washington

Ostendorf collection

NEGRO FRIENDS OF LINCOLN

Top left: WILLIAM FLORVILLE ("Billy the Barber") was a light-complexioned Negro from Haiti. He cut Lincoln's hair for years, and Lincoln helped him with his tax problems. *Top right:* MARIAH VANCE (Mrs. Henry Vance) worked twice weekly as cook and washerwoman for the Lincolns from 1850 to 1861. Shortly before her death in 1904 she dictated her memoirs, still unpublished. *Bottom left:* ELIZABETH KECKLEY, companion and seamstress to the First Lady, collaborated with James Redpath in 1868 to write *Behind the Scenes at the White House.* *Bottom right:* WILLIAM SLADE, a personal friend and valet to the President, often acted as a confidential messenger. He supervised the other White House Negro help and accompanied Lincoln to Gettysburg in 1863.

Illinois State Historical Library   Ostendorf collection   Illinois State Historical Library

HIS OUTSTANDING RIVALS—SOME WERE ALSO HIS FRIENDS

Left: JOHN J. HARDIN wrested the Illinois Whig candidacy from Lincoln and was elected to Congress in 1834 where he served one term. He became a general in the Mexican War and was killed at the head of his regiment in the Battle of Buena Vista. *Center:* EDWARD D. BAKER followed Hardin to Congress on the Whig ticket and, by agreement with Lincoln, served only a single term, after which Lincoln was nominated and elected. Although Baker was a political rival, Lincoln became his fast friend and named his second son after him. *Right:* GENERAL JAMES T. SHIELDS, a distinguished army officer and politician, claimed that Lincoln had maligned him in newspaper articles and challenged him to a duel. Lincoln chose large cavalry broadswords to be wielded over a plank set edgewise in the ground, but at the last moment both men were talked out of a fight in which Shields would have been at the mercy of his long-armed adversary.

Left: JEFFERSON DAVIS was president of the Confederacy. Like Lincoln, he was born in Kentucky and was a veteran of the Black Hawk War. *Right:* ALEXANDER H. STEPHENS impressed Lincoln tremendously with his intellect and eloquence when both were serving in Congress. Although Stephens opposed secession, he accepted the post of vice-president of the Confederacy.

Ostendorf collection   Ostendorf collection

All photographs Ostendorf collection

OPPONENTS FOR THE PRESIDENCY
LINCOLN'S BIGGEST POLITICAL RIVALS IN 1860

Left: STEPHEN A. DOUGLAS, candidate of the northern and western Democrats, who insured Lincoln's election when he split the Democratic ranks. *Center:* JOHN BELL, nominee of the Constitutional Union party, a group of alarmed conservatives. *Right:* JOHN C. BRECKENRIDGE, leader of the Southern Democrats, a party composed of slaveholders and anti-Douglas men.

Right: GEORGE B. McCLELLAN, former general-in-chief of the Union Army, was the Democratic choice to oppose Lincoln on a "stop-the-war" platform. Union successes just before the election helped give Lincoln a landslide victory. McClellan lost the 1864 election to Lincoln by an electoral vote of 212 to 21.

Photograph by Brady in National Archives

Carte-de-visite photograph
by Brady, Ostendorf collection

LINCOLN'S PREDECESSOR

O-94

Above, left: JAMES BUCHANAN, outgoing President, looked tired and woebegone when, after four years of vacillation and compromise, he turned over his great office to Lincoln. Buchanan had failed utterly to meet the challenge of South Carolina's secession. *Left:* ABRAHAM LINCOLN, the new President, was determined to fight, if necessary, to save the Union. In the Presidency he saw "a task before me greater than that which rested upon Washington." *Above, right:* HANNIBAL HAMLIN, Lincoln's first vice-president, missed becoming the nation's leader by only six weeks. Had Booth carried out his earlier plans to kill Lincoln, Hamlin would have been the seventeenth President.

348

Ostendorf collection   O–88

Ostendorf collection

LINCOLN'S SUCCESSOR

SEATED IN THE IDENTICAL CHAIR in Brady's studio, Lincoln and his second vice-president Andrew Johnson form an interesting contrast in profiles. Unlike most notables of his day, Lincoln never affected the Napoleonic hand-in-vest pose.

ANDREW JOHNSON (left), who succeeded Lincoln, began his career as a tailor's apprentice and did not learn to read or write until manhood. As President, he tried valiantly to carry out Lincoln's plan "to bind up the nation's wounds," but a vengeful Congress impeached him. He was acquitted by one vote. This photograph of Johnson was taken by W. Snell, of the Whitehurst gallery, Pennsylvania Avenue, Washington, D. C.

Ostendorf collection

349

CAMERON   STANTON   SEWARD

LINCOLN'S OFFICIAL FAMILY

LINCOLN'S TWO SECRETARIES OF WAR were Simon Cameron (above, left), wealthy, unctuous, and wily, who resigned early in 1862 after his manner of awarding army contracts was severely criticized; and Edwin M. Stanton (above, center), tough and impolitic, on whose competent shoulders Lincoln placed much of the burden of the war effort.

William H. Seward (above, right) was secretary of state during the entire Lincoln administration. A brilliant and capricious politician, he expected to be the brains behind Lincoln. Eventually he filled his own post with great skill. Gideon Welles (right), humorless and grumpy, served as secretary of the navy throughout the entire war. His huge white beard and thick brown wig made him appear like a venerable detective wearing false whiskers.

All photographs Ostendorf collection

WELLES

350

CHASE   FESSENDEN   McCULLOCH

LINCOLN'S FIRST SECRETARY OF THE TREASURY was Salmon P. Chase. Honest and ambitious, he had hoped for the Presidency himself. When his aspirations fizzled out in 1864, he resigned and was appointed chief justice of the United States Supreme Court by the man he tried to supplant. William P. Fessenden, a former United States senator and one of Lincoln's most ardent supporters, was secretary of the treasury from July 1, 1864, to March 3, 1865, when he resigned to return to the Senate. Hugh McCulloch, who had served for two years as United States comptroller of the currency, accepted the post of secretary of the treasury on March 9, 1865 and served with the Lincoln administration for little more than a month.

All photographs Ostendorf collection

351

BATES   SPEED
LINCOLN'S OFFICIAL FAMILY

THE FIRST ATTORNEY GENERAL in Lincoln's administration was Edward Bates
(left), a pensive, unimaginative man. A stuffy lawyer of the old school, he resigned in 1864 because of old age. James Speed (right) became Lincoln's attorney general in December, 1864. A skilled attorney whose efforts had helped
to keep Kentucky in the Union, he was a brother of Lincoln's most intimate
friend, Joshua Speed of Springfield.

All photographs Ostendorf collection

DENNISON

LINCOLN'S FIRST POSTMASTER GENERAL was Montgomery Blair (right). Clever and influential, he was a leader of the Union element in Maryland. His caustic remarks led to friction in the cabinet. William Dennison (left) became postmaster general in October, 1864, after Blair was forced to resign. A former governor of Ohio, Dennison was soft and politic, an excellent choice for a post requiring great diplomacy.

BLAIR

SMITH

SECRETARY OF THE INTERIOR from March 5, 1861, until January 1, 1863, was Caleb B. Smith (left), a colorless Indiana politician. The post had been promised to him by Judge Davis before the election. John P. Usher (right) succeeded Smith as secretary of the interior. A former assistant in the department, he was an old friend of Lincoln and a devoted Republican.

All photographs Ostendorf collection

USHER

A CHRONOLOGICAL SEQUENCE OF
LINCOLN PHOTOGRAPHS
COMPILED BY LLOYD OSTENDORF

A PRESENTATION of all the photographs of Lincoln known to exist almost a century after his death.

Each picture is identified with its Ostendorf (O) number and its Meserve (M) number, if one exists; and, when known, with the date and place and the name of the photographer.

Included are accounts of seventeen Lincoln camera portraits which were lost or destroyed.

"THESE CAMERAS," observed Lincoln during a visit to Brady's gallery, "are painfully truthful." Yet the Civil War President owned at least two photograph albums, one of which was noted by Carl Schurz when he visited the Springfield home in May, 1860, and another, more battered, which Lincoln dubbed his "rogues gallery" and presented to his Negro maid. Doubtless these albums held many of the portraits which appear in this book, for Lincoln realized the historic value of his photographs and was careful to save them.

From the time of the Douglas debates until his death, the former railsplitter with the gnarled face intrigued both the public and the cameramen. He was much in demand at the galleries. Once during his 1860 tour he forgot about a promised sitting for Beers and Mansfield in New Haven. On his return to Springfield he wrote an apology, adding that he meant "no intentional disrespect."

Many well-known galleries pleaded in vain for a sitting. On January 30, 1864, Bell and Brothers of Washington asked Lincoln to pose, assuring him that "you will find yourself with warm friends, and we will furnish you with proof of our skill as photographers." The President was evidently too busy, for there is no record that he visited their gallery.

Lincoln did pose for at least seventeen photographs, now lost or destroyed—eight of them in fires. And there are legends which tell of many other sittings. A newspaper story described a daguerreotype taken in Bloomington in 1846 which showed Lincoln "seated on an old rush-bottomed chair; common suit of

354

dark color; wearing an old-fashioned stock and turned-down collar, hair un-combed, standing up in all directions and his right hand holding a letter. It was taken for Dr. William Hobbs, a warm friend." It is said, too—and Meserve is our authority for this one—that Lincoln and his secretary of state, William H. Seward, were photographed together by Brady.

The Lincolns' Negro maid, Mariah Vance, claimed that she once owned a group picture of Mr. and Mrs. Lincoln with their son Robert, a standing pose which because of the comic disparity in heights was not liked by the family. "That photographer sure mixed us up," commented Lincoln, in presenting Mariah with the picture. Before her death in 1904, this family portrait disap-peared. It is possible that Mariah's memory of it was confused, for Robert Todd Lincoln told Meserve that his father and mother were never photographed together.

The tales of missing Lincoln photographs even include some taken after his death. There is a possibility that an Indianapolis photographer, perhaps George Koch, took a picture of Lincoln in his casket on Sunday, April 30, 1865. And in 1952 a descendant of a Chicago cameraman claimed to own a photograph of the dead President taken in Chicago on Monday, May 1, 1865.

When a "new" Lincoln photograph turns up, it must pass certain tests. Sev-eral years ago the picture of a tall bearded man in a top hat was identified as "Lincoln in New Hampshire." But Lincoln was never on the Contoocook River in Peterborough, where the picture was taken; and when he toured New Hampshire in 1860, he was beardless. It is by such evidence that many photo-graphs are condemned as fakes.

Even more difficult is the problem of establishing the time and place of those photographs which are found to be genuine. There are many guides. Lincoln's face, hair, beard, clothing—all are helpful. The type of photograph and the gallery props and furnishings may also suggest a date.

The earliest-recorded photograph of Lincoln was taken in 1846 when the thirty-seven-year-old lawyer was elected to Congress. Photography was then only seven years old. There were already two daguerreotypists in Lincoln's home town—N. H. Shepherd, who took the first-known picture of the future President, and William R. Williams of Cincinnati, who operated the National Daguerrian Gallery. But itinerant photographers may have visited Springfield long before 1846. The earliest possible date for a photograph of Lincoln is 1840, the year the daguerreotype was introduced to America and the year in which the first traveling cameramen reached the cities of the West. The latest possible date is April, 1865, the month Lincoln was murdered. Thus all Lincoln photographs, known or unknown, must be placed within a span of twenty-five years.

The type of photograph may suggest its date. From the invention of the camera in 1839 until about 1855, the daguerreotype (on silvered copper) was in vogue. It was succeeded by the ambrotype (on glass), which was in favor until about 1859, when the tintype and carte-de-visite (a paper photograph printed in sepia and pasted on a card) became popular. Most of the available photographs of Lincoln are cartes-de-visite made after 1860.

Sometimes the color tints of an old photograph can help fix its date. The earliest daguerreotypes, ambrotypes, and tintypes often had hand-tinted cheeks and lips. A revenue stamp on the back of a photograph provides a further clue, for these two-cent stamps were required only during the period between September 1, 1864, and August 1, 1866.

Many cameramen posed their sitters near draperies with cords and tassels, pedestals or podiums, marble-top tables, and ornate chairs. Such props, like the pattern on the carpet or floor, often differed from gallery to gallery and thus help to fix the name of the photographer and the place where he took the picture. Frequently, too, studio props establish that a portrait is, or is not, one of a series taken at a certain sitting.

The mole on Lincoln's right cheek, usually visible in unretouched photographs, is the check point to determine whether a portrait has been printed in reverse. To the viewer, the mole should appear on the left side of the face.

Lincoln wore short sideburns in the 1840's, but by the late 1850's he was clean-shaven. In October, 1860, he started to grow the beard which he kept for the rest of his life. Any photograph showing Lincoln without a beard was taken before November, 1860; any unretouched picture of him with whiskers was taken after October, 1860.

Lincoln generally wore his hair long, but early in 1865 it was cut very short. Usually he parted it on the left, but some of the photographs taken in 1864 show his part on the right side. For several weeks in May, 1860, Lincoln experimented with a rude pompadour.

His type of tie and collar may furnish an important clue, but this method of dating is not entirely reliable. Fashions were not so changeable in Lincoln's day, and he often dressed in out-of-date shirts and ties. In the early portraits he appears mainly in large bow ties and stock collars, but some early pictures show small ties and turned-down collars. As candidate for the Presidency, Lincoln usually wore a shorter tie. During his first year in the White House he favored a high, overlapping collar, but he subsequently adopted a lower collar which he stuck with until his death.

Portraits often turn up with his face much altered by the manicuring of the beard and hair or the addition of false whiskers, or with the imprint of a gallery not known to have photographed Lincoln. Since most fabricators and photograph-pirates did not bother to change the tie and collar on the original, a careful comparison with the ties and collars on all of the photographs in the Ostendorf chronology will show whether a picture is a new, unknown pose or merely an old face retouched or issued under a new imprint.

The quest for new Lincoln photographs goes on. Lured by rumors and hints, collectors continue to ransack cellars and attics, trunks and old albums. Scholars pour over files of libraries and historical societies searching for photographs which *might* exist. Why is there no pose of Lincoln with any member of his cabinet? Or with his great opponent of the debates, Stephen A. Douglas? And why is there no photograph of Lincoln with his wife? Or with his son Robert? Or with his greatest general, U. S. Grant?

To discover any of these unknown poses or turn up any of the missing pictures described in story and legend is the hope which inspires the endless search for new Lincoln photographs.

1846   (M–1) O–1
Daguerreotype by N. H. Shepherd,
Springfield, 1846.

1857   (M–6) O–2
Photograph by Alexander Hesler, Chicago, Saturday, February 28, 1857.

1857   (M–2) O–3
Ambrotype by Amon T. Joslin, Danville,
Wednesday, May 27, 1857.

1858   (M–5) O–4
Ambrotype by Samuel G. Alschuler, Urbana, Sunday, April 25, 1858.

359

1858   (M–7)   O–5
Ambrotype by Abraham M. Byers,
Beardstown, Friday, May 7, 1858.

1858   (M–3)   O–6
Daguerreotype by P. Von Schneidau,
Chicago, Sunday, July 11, 1858.

1858   (M–17)   O–7
Ambrotype by Preston Butler, Springfield, July 18, 1858.

1858   (M–10)   O–8
Ambrotype by T. P. Pearson, Macomb,
Thursday, August 26, 1858.

1858   (M–9)   O–9
Photograph, probably by C. S. German,
Springfield, Sunday, September 26, 1858.

1858   (M–12)   O–10
Ambrotype by Calvin Jackson, Pittsfield,
Friday, October 1, 1858.

1858

Destroyed ambrotype by Calvin Jackson,
Pittsfield, Illinois, Friday, October 1,
1858.

At the request of attorney D. H. Gilmer, who wished to have a portrait of
him, Lincoln posed for two ambrotypes
in the gallery of Calvin Jackson at Pittsfield, Illinois, on October 1, 1858. The
surviving picture (O–10) is very dark,
giving Lincoln's complexion a black and
leathery appearance. Possibly the second
ambrotype, taken at the same sitting, was
even more underexposed and was destroyed by either the photographer or
Lincoln.

1858   (M–13)   O–11
Ambrotype by William Judkins Thompson, Monmouth, Monday, October 11,
1858.

1858 (M–4) O–12
Tintype, cameraman, date, and place unknown. Probably 1858.

1858 (M–117) O–13
Photograph, cameraman, date, and place unknown. Probably 1858.

1858 (M–14) O–14
Ambrotype, probably by Roderick M. Cole, Peoria, Illinois, probably 1858.

1859 (M–32) O–15
Photograph, cameraman unknown, probably in Springfield. Probably 1859.

1859
Lost daguerreotype, by an unknown cameraman, Columbus, Ohio, *Friday*, September 16, 1859.

The Columbus *Statesman*, a paper which opposed Lincoln's political views, reported: "We think Mr. Lincoln will never be invited here again, and that was perhaps his opinion, as he had his daguerreotype taken in the forenoon, with a view of leaving it, we suppose, as a remembrancer for his Columbus friends. It ought to be hung in the Young Men's Republican Club room."

1859
Destroyed daguerreotype by Thomas Walker Cridland, Dayton, Ohio, *Saturday*, September 17, 1859.

The grandson of photographer Cridland, Walter D. McKinney, wrote: "My grandfather was introduced to Mr. Lincoln by Samuel Craighead . . . and Lincoln accompanied Mr. Cridland to the photographic gallery, where photographs were made. . . . the negative, or negatives, were destroyed by a fire about 1865 in the attic of the gallery. . . . "I well remember the destruction of the original negative as told over and over again."

1859   (M–8) O–16
Photograph by Samuel M. Fassett, Chicago, Tuesday, October 4, 1859.

1860   (M–20) O–17
Photograph by Mathew B. Brady, New York, Monday, February 27, 1860.

1860   (M–110)   O–18

Photograph, cameraman unknown, Chicago, probably *Wednesday*, April 4, 1860.

1860   (M–122)   O–19

Photograph by Edward A. Barnwell, Decatur, Wednesday, May 9, 1860.

1860   (M–22)   O–20

Photograph by William Marsh, Springfield, Sunday, May 20, 1860.

1860   (M–21)   O–21

Photograph by William Marsh, Springfield, Sunday, May 20, 1860.

1860   (M–109)   O–22
Ambrotype, probably by William Marsh,
Springfield, Thursday, May 24, 1860.

1860   O–23
Ambrotype, probably by William Marsh,
Springfield, Thursday, May 24, 1860.

1860
Destroyed photographs (four) by Pres-
ton Butler, Springfield, Illinois, Saturday,
May 26, 1860.

The Chicago sculptor, Leonard Wells
Volk, at work on a statue of Lincoln,
journeyed to Springfield to make casts of
Lincoln's hands. He was presented with a
black alpaca suit and a pair of pegged
boots which Lincoln had worn during
the debates with Douglas. Then he persuaded Lincoln to pose at Butler's studio,
where, on May 26, 1860, four full-length
negatives were taken: "front, rear, and
two flanks." These photographs, together
with Lincoln's suit and boots, were
burned in the Chicago fire of 1871.

1860   (M–124)   O–24
Photograph, probably by William Marsh,
Springfield, May, 1860.

365

Destroyed photographs (three) by Joseph Hill, Springfield, June, 1860.

Soon after Lincoln's nomination for the Presidency, photographer Joseph Hill of Galesburg traveled to Springfield to take some pictures of the candidate. He took four pictures, one of them a full-length seated portrait showing Lincoln's 18-inch boots. All the negative plates were destroyed later in a studio fire. Only a discarded print of the previous picture (O–25) survived the flames.

1860   (M–102)   O–25
Photograph by Joseph Hill, Springfield, June, 1860.

1860   (M–26)   O–26
Photograph by Alexander Hesler, Springfield, *Sunday*, June 3, 1860.

1860   (M–25)   O–27
Photograph by Alexander Hesler, Springfield, *Sunday*, June 3, 1860.

1860   (M–28)   O–28

Photograph by Alexander Hesler, Springfield, *Sunday*, June 3, 1860.

1860   (M–27)   O–29

Photograph by Alexander Hesler, Springfield, *Sunday*, June 3, 1860.

1860   (M–112)   O–30

Photograph by William Seavy, Springfield, Summer, 1860.

1860   (M–111)   O–31

Photograph, by an unknown cameraman,
Springfield, Summer, 1860.

1860   (M–31)   O–32
Photograph, by an unknown cameraman,
Springfield, probably June, 1860.

1860   (M–113)   O–33
Photograph, by an unknown cameraman,
Springfield, about June, 1860.

1860   (M–16)   O–34
Photograph, by an unknown cameraman,
Springfield, Wednesday, August 8, 1860.

1860   (M–120)   O–35
Photograph, by an unknown cameraman,
Springfield, Summer, 1860.

1860 (M–29) O–36
Ambrotype by Preston Butler, Springfield, Monday, August 13, 1860.

1860 (M–30) O–37
Ambrotype by Preston Butler, Springfield, Monday, August 13, 1860.

1860
Lost ambrotypes (four) by Preston Butler, Springfield, Monday, August 13,
1860.

The diary of artist John Henry Brown,
for whom Preston Butler took the two
previous ambrotypes (O–36 and O–37),
reveals that four more poses of Lincoln
were made on the same day. "He at
once consented to sit for his picture.
We walked together from the Executive
Chamber to a daguerrean establishment.
I had a half dozen ambrotypes taken of
him before I could get one to suit me."

These four missing ambrotypes bring
to a total of eight (see page 365) the portraits by Preston Butler which were lost
or destroyed.

1860 (M–23) O–38
Photograph by J. A. Whipple, Springfield, Summer, 1860.

1860 (M–24) O–39
Photograph by J. A. Whipple, Springfield, Summer, 1860.

THE EVOLUTION OF LINCOLN'S BEARD is an interesting study. By the time of his inauguration on March 4, 1861, his whiskers were full-grown and imposingly thick. The beard remained heavy until early in 1863 when it began a gradual transformation. Month by month the White House barbers clipped and trimmed until, in the final months of his life, it was little more than a five-o'clock shadow.

1860   (M–33)   O–40
Photograph by Samuel G. Alschuler, Chicago, Sunday, November 25, 1860.

1861   (M–34)   O–41
Photograph by Christopher S. German, Springfield, Sunday, January 13, 1861.

1861   O–42
Photograph by Christopher S. German, Springfield, Sunday, January 13, 1861.

1861

Lost photograph (type unknown), cameraman unknown, Clyde, New York, Monday, February 18, 1861.

According to a *New York Times* reporter, a photographer had set up his camera on a woodpile near the train tracks so that he could take a picture of the President-elect when the train stopped at the canal port of Clyde for five minutes (8:44 to 8:49 A.M.). The *New York Times* and the *Buffalo Express* stated that the photographer got "pictures of the rear end of the car, of Mr. Lincoln, Mr. Wood, a brakeman and a . . . reporter."

These pictures have never been found.

1861   (M–35) O–43
Photograph by Christopher S. German, Springfield, Saturday, February 9, 1861.

1861   (M–36) O–44
Photograph by Christopher S. German, Springfield, Saturday, February 9, 1861.

1861   O–45
Photograph by Christopher S. German, Springfield, Saturday, February 9, 1861.

373

1861   O–46
Photograph by F. DeB. Richards, Philadelphia, Pennsylvania, Friday, February
22, 1861.

1861   (M–103)   O–47
Photograph by F. DeB. Richards, Philadelphia, Pennsylvania, Friday, February
22, 1861.

1861   (M–37)   O–48
Photograph by F. DeB. Richards, Philadelphia, Pennsylvania, Friday, February
22, 1861.

1861   (M–71)   O–49
Photograph by Alexander Gardner at
M. B. Brady's gallery, Washington, D. C.,
Sunday, February 24, 1861.

1861   (M–68, M–118) O–50
Photograph by Alexander Gardner at
M. B. Brady's gallery, Washington, D. C.,
Sunday, February 24, 1861.

1861   (M–72) O–51
Photograph by Alexander Gardner at
M. B. Brady's gallery, Washington, D. C.,
Sunday, February 24, 1861.

1861   (M–69) O–52
Photograph by Alexander Gardner at
M. B. Brady's gallery, Washington, D. C.,
Sunday, February 24, 1861.

1861   (M–70) O–53
Photograph by Alexander Gardner at
M. B. Brady's gallery, Washington, D. C.,
Sunday, February 24, 1861.

1861   O–54
Photograph, by an unknown cameraman, Washington, D. C., Monday, March 4, 1861.

1861   (M–42)   O–55
Photograph, by an unknown cameraman, Washington, D. C., taken before June 30, 1861.

1861   O–56
Photograph by Edward Bierstadt, Washington or vicinity, September, 1861.

1861   (M–66)   O–57
Photograph by Mathew B. Brady, Washington, D. C., probably 1862.

1862   (M–65)   O–58
Photograph by Mathew B. Brady, Washington, D. C., 1862.

1862   (M–67)   O–59
Photograph by Mathew B. Brady, Washington, D. C., 1862.

1862   (M–64)   O–60
Photograph by Mathew B. Brady, Washington, D. C., 1862.

1862   (M–63)   O–61
Photograph by Mathew B. Brady, Washington, D. C., 1862.

1862　　　　　　(M–44)　O–62
Photograph by Alexander Gardner, Antietam, Maryland, Friday, October 3,
1862.

1862　　　　　　(M–46)　O–63
Photograph by Alexander Gardner, Antietam, Maryland, Friday, October 3,
1862.

1862　　　　　　(M–45)　O–64
Photograph by Alexander Gardner, Antietam, Maryland, Friday, October 3,
1862.

1862　　　　　　(M–47)　O–65
Photograph by Alexander Gardner, Antietam, Maryland, Friday, October 3,
1862.

378

1862   (M–43)   O–66
Photograph by Alexander Gardner, Antietam, Maryland, Friday, October 3, 1862.

1862   (M–123) O–67
Photograph by Alexander Gardner, Antietam, Maryland, Friday, October 3, 1862.

1862   (M–A)   O–68
Photograph by O. Pierre Havens, Virginia, about 1862 or 1863.

1863   (M–38)   O–69
Photograph by Thomas Le Mere at Brady's gallery, Washington, D. C., Friday, April 17, 1863.

1863   (M–53) O–70
Photograph by Alexander Gardner,
Washington, D. C., Sunday, August 9,
1863.

1863   (M–51, M–52) O–71
Photograph by Alexander Gardner,
Washington, D. C., Sunday, August 9,
1863.

1863   (M–54) O–72
Photograph by Alexander Gardner,
Washington, D. C., Sunday, August 9,
1863.

1863   (M–49, M–50) O–73
Photograph by Alexander Gardner,
Washington, D. C., Sunday, August 9,
1863.

1863 (M–55) O–74
Photograph by Alexander Gardner, Washington, D. C., Sunday, August 9, 1863.

1863 (M–105) O–75
Photograph by Alexander Gardner, Washington, D. C., Sunday, August 9, 1863.

1863 (M–56) O–76
Photograph by Alexander Gardner, Washington, D. C., Sunday, November 8, 1863.

1863 (M–59) O–77
Photograph by Alexander Gardner, Washington, D. C., Sunday, November 8, 1863.

1863   (M–57, M–60) O–78
Photograph by Alexander Gardner, Washington, D. C., Sunday, November 8, 1863.

1863   (M–58) O–79
Photograph by Alexander Gardner, Washington, D. C., Sunday, November 8, 1863.

1863   (M–61) O–80
Photograph by Alexander Gardner, Washington, D. C., Sunday, November 8, 1863.

1863   (M–129) O–81
Photograph by unidentified assistant of Mathew B. Brady, Gettysburg, Pennsylvania, Thursday, November 19, 1863.

1863   (M–88) O–82
Photograph by Lewis E. Walker, Washington, D. C., 1863.

1864   (M–73, M–74) O–83
Photograph by Mathew B. Brady, Washington, D. C., Friday, January 8, 1864.

1864   (M–75) O–84
Photograph by Mathew B. Brady, Washington, D. C., Friday, January 8, 1864.

1864   (M–78) O–85
Photograph by Mathew B. Brady, Washington, D. C., Friday, January 8, 1864.

1864   (M–76)   O–86
Photograph by Mathew B. Brady, Washington, D. C., Friday, January 8, 1864.

1864   (M–77)   O–87
Photograph by Mathew B. Brady, Washington, D. C., Friday, January 8, 1864.

1864   (M–81, M–82, M–83)   O–88
Photograph by Anthony Berger at Brady's Washington gallery, Tuesday, February 9, 1864.

1864   (M–84)   O–89
Photograph by Anthony Berger at Brady's Washington gallery, Tuesday, February 9, 1864.

1864   (M–86)   O–90

Photograph by Anthony Berger at Brady's Washington gallery, Tuesday, February 9, 1864.

1864   O–91

Photograph by Anthony Berger at Brady's Washington gallery, Tuesday, February 9, 1864.

1864   (M–85)   O–92

Photograph by Anthony Berger at Brady's Washington gallery, Tuesday, February 9, 1864.

1864   (M–127)   O–93

Photograph by Anthony Berger at Brady's Washington gallery, Tuesday, February 9, 1864.

1864   (M–119) O–94
Photograph by Anthony Berger at Brady's Washington gallery, Tuesday, February 9, 1864.

1864   (M–97) O–95
Photograph by Wenderoth & Taylor, Washington, D. C., 1864.

1864   (M–80) O–96
Photograph by Wenderoth & Taylor, Washington, D. C., 1864.

1864   (M–121) O–97
Photograph by Anthony Berger at Brady's Washington gallery, Wednesday, April 20, 1864.

386

1864   O-98

Photograph by Anthony Berger at Brady's Washington gallery, Wednesday, April 20, 1864.

1864   O-99

Photograph by Anthony Berger at Brady's Washington gallery, Wednesday, April 20, 1864.

1864   (M-106) O-100

Photograph by Anthony Berger at the White House, Washington, D. C., Tuesday, April 26, 1864.

1864   (M-128) O-101

Photograph by Anthony Berger at the White House, Washington, D. C., Tuesday, April 26, 1864.

1864   (M–116)   O–102
Photograph by Anthony Berger at White
House, Washington, D. C., Tuesday,
April 26, 1864.

1865   (M–92)   O–103
Photograph by E. & H. T. Anthony Co.,
Washington, D. C., February, 1865.

1865   (M–91)   O–104
Photograph by E. & H. T. Anthony Co.,
Washington, D. C., February, 1865.

1865   O–105
Photograph, cameraman unknown, possibly Gardner, Washington, D. C., Saturday, March 4, 1865.

1865 (M–89) O–106
Photograph, cameraman unknown, possibly Gardner, Washington, D. C., Saturday, March 4, 1865.

1865 O–107
Photograph by William Morris Smith, Washington, D. C., Saturday, March 4, 1865.

1865 (M–90) O–108
Photograph, cameraman unknown, possibly Gardner, Washington, D. C., Saturday, March 4, 1865.

1865 O–109
Photograph, by an unknown cameraman, Washington, D. C., Saturday, March 4, 1865.

1865   O-110
Photograph, by an unknown cameraman,
Washington, D. C., Saturday, March 4,
1865.

1865   O-111
Photograph, by an unknown cameraman,
Washington, D. C., Saturday, March 4,
1865.

1865   (M-93)   O-112
Photograph by Henry F. Warren, White
House balcony, Washington, D. C., Mon-
day, March 6, 1865.

1865   O-113
Photograph by Henry F. Warren, White
House balcony, Washington, D. C., Mon-
day, March 6, 1865.

1865
Lost photograph by Henry F. Warren, White House balcony, Monday, March 6, 1865.

It was recorded that Warren "made three pictures of Mr. Lincoln, one standing, and two sitting." The two seated poses (O–112 and O–113) were made on a chair which Lincoln himself carried out on the balcony, but the standing pose has never come to light.

After Warren's death, according to friends, his collection of negatives changed hands several times. Its present location is not known.

1865   (M–95)   O–114
Photograph by Alexander Gardner, Washington, D. C., Monday, April 10, 1865.

1865   (M–99)   O–115
Photograph by Alexander Gardner, Washington, D. C., Monday, April 10, 1865.

1865   (M–97)   O–116
Photograph by Alexander Gardner, Washington, D. C., Monday, April 10, 1865.

1865   (M–98)   O–117
Photograph by Alexander Gardner, Washington, D. C., Monday, April 10, 1865.

1865   (M–100)   O–118
Photograph by Alexander Gardner, Washington, D. C., Monday, April 10, 1865.

1865
Destroyed photographs by Jeremiah Gurney of Gurney and Son, Governor's room of the New York City Hall, Monday, April 24, 1865.

At the cost of "much time and labor," Gurney took two photographs of the body of Lincoln as it lay in state. On the orders of Secretary of War Edwin M. Stanton, who claimed that Mrs. Lincoln objected to the pictures, negatives and prints were confiscated. However, among his papers Stanton preserved a single small print (O–119) from the four-lens plate. Both negative and all the prints from a larger view were destroyed.

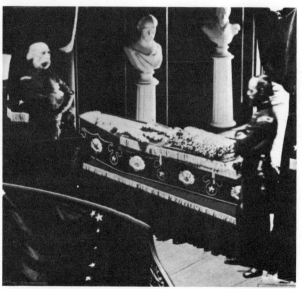

1865   (M–130)   O–119
Photograph by Jeremiah Gurney, Jr., New York City, Monday, April 24, 1865.

THE PHOTOGRAPHERS OF LINCOLN
A STATISTICAL SURVEY

ALTHOUGH BRADY HIMSELF is credited with only eleven pictures of Lincoln, many by Alexander Gardner and all of those by Anthony Berger were posed at Brady's gallery or under his direction. Thomas Le Mere, another Brady operator, also photographed the Civil War President.

Among other Brady employees and associates who may at times have assisted in taking Lincoln's picture are James Gardner, Timothy H. O'Sullivan, Lewis H. Landy, David B. Woodbury, John Reckie, Thomas C. Roche, John Wood, George N. Barnard, J. F. Coonley, Sam F. Cooley, William R. Pywell, David Knox, Stanley Morrow, James F. Gibson, James Wright, George G. Rockwood, Egbert Guy Faux, A. B. Foons, H. Moulton, T. Brown, R. Meyers, B. Myers, and Ide Banes, a positioner at Brady's.

Wartime assistants of Alexander Gardner were his brother James, Samuel Ott, S. F. Denny, and William Morris Smith, some of whom may also have worked for Brady.

Photographers of Lincoln	No. of Photos	No. of Sittings	Place Where Photographed
N. H. Shepherd	1	1	Springfield, Illinois
Alexander Hesler	5	2	Springfield & Chicago, Illinois
Amon T. Joslin	1	1	Danville, Illinois
Samuel G. Alschuler	2	2	Urbana & Chicago, Illinois
Abraham M. Byers	2	1	Beardstown, Illinois
Polycarp Von Schneidau	1	1	Chicago, Illinois
Preston Butler	11	3	Springfield, Illinois
Christopher S. German	5	3	Springfield, Illinois
T. Painter Pearson	1	1	Macomb, Illinois
Calvin Jackson	2	1	Pittsfield, Illinois
William Judkins Thompson	1	1	Monmouth, Illinois
Roderick M. Cole	1	1	Peoria, Illinois
Thomas Walker Cridland	1	1	Dayton, Ohio
Samuel M. Fassett	1	1	Chicago, Illinois
Mathew B. Brady	11	3	New York & Washington, D. C.
Thomas Le Mere	1	1	Washington, D. C.
Edward A. Barnwell	1	1	Decatur, Illinois
William Marsh	5	3	Springfield, Illinois
Joseph Hill	4	1	Springfield, Illinois
John Adams Whipple	2	1	Springfield, Illinois
Lewis E. Walker	1	1	Washington, D. C.
William Seavy	1	1	Springfield, Illinois
F. DeBourg Richards	3	1	Philadelphia, Pennsylvania
Wenderoth & Taylor	2	1	Washington, D. C.
Alexander Gardner	30	6	Washington, D. C. & Antietam, Maryland
Edward Bierstadt	1	1	Washington, D. C.
E. & H. T. Anthony Co.	2	1	Washington, D. C.
William Morris Smith	1	1	Washington, D. C.
Henry F. Warren	3	1	Washington, D. C.
Anthony Berger	13	3	Washington, D. C.
O. Pierre Havens	1	1	Virginia
Jeremiah Gurney	2	(death)	New York, N. Y.
Unknown	16	13	Washington, D. C. Springfield, Illinois Columbus, Ohio Chicago, Illinois Clyde, New York Gettysburg, Pennsylvania

ACKNOWLEDGMENTS

IN THE COMPILATION AND WRITING OF THIS BOOK the authors have incurred a great debt to Lincoln scholars and collectors for their enthusiastic co-operation in lending photographs and supplying historical data.

Of the greatest value was the aid and encouragement of the distinguished collector, Frederick Hill Meserve of New York, who placed no reservations upon the use of his vast Lincoln photograph collection and was equally generous with his time and suggestions. The dedication of this volume to Meserve is an acknowledgment of the immense debt owed to him, not merely by the writers of this book, but by all who are interested in the photographic history of the nineteenth century.

From Lincoln's own state the aid of scholars and experts was of inestimable help. Thanks are due to Paul M. Angle, and Mrs. Paul H. Rhymer of the Chicago Historical Society; the late distinguished authority, Harry E. Pratt; Mrs. Marion Dolores Pratt and Miss Margaret A. Flint, of Springfield, as well as Ralph G. Newman of Chicago. Among others who generously offered their help were James T. Hickey, curator of the Lincoln collection in the Illinois Historical Library at Springfield, who furnished both pictures and pertinent facts to go with them; the late Ernest E. East, of Springfield; Bruce E. Wheeler, Lincolniana editor of *Hobbies*, in Chicago; and Clyde C. Walton, Illinois state historian.

To the Library of Congress and its staff the authors are especially grateful. Josephine Cobb, formerly archivist in charge of the Still Picture Branch of the National Archives, and now iconography specialist with the same institution, offered valuable suggestions on the work of Brady and Gardner and allowed Lloyd Ostendorf to study at first hand the contemporary collodion plates in the Brady collection. Others from the Library of Congress who were helpful are David C. Mearns, Hirst Milhollen, Carl Stange, and Virginia Daiker.

Much appreciated, also, was the co-operation of Edgar C. Cox and Mrs. Alice Handy Cox, proprietors of the L. C. Handy studio, successor to Brady. The assistance of those experts on photography, Beaumont Newhall, curator of George Eastman House in Rochester and Fredrick S. Lightfoot of Hollis, New York, is gratefully acknowledged. Special thanks go to Emerson Carpenter Ives of Pawling, New York. Other experts who contributed their time and knowledge are Arthur Carlson of the New-York Historical Society and the late Benjamin P. Thomas, noted biographer of Lincoln.

A particular debt of gratitude is due to those who provided pictures. King V. Hostick of Chicago for his encouragement and generous permission to publish his important, newly discovered photograph of Lincoln's second inaugural. Carl Haverlin of New York; the New York Public Library; and Tom Lamberson and Harry Golden of Richmond, Indiana, deserve special mention. The authors are grateful to those who furnished not only photographs but important data about the Lincoln family, among whom are Ada L. Sutton of Attica, Indiana; Adin Baber of Kansas, Illinois, authority on the Hanks family; and William S. Orr of Batavia, New York. Information on the Lincoln family was also furnished by Charles H. Lincoln of Taunton, Massachusetts.

Further aid came from Wayne C. Temple and the late Robert L. Kincaid, both of the Lincoln Memorial University at Harrogate, Tennessee; and Larry L. Belles, executive director of the Harlin-Lincoln Commission in Iowa.

Philip D. Sang of Chicago generously offered the use of his collections and even brought his file of Lincoln photographs by plane to New York for the authors' examination; Cornelius Greenway and Philip Van Doren Stern, both of Brooklyn, New York, were most helpful. Louis A. Warren, director emeritus, and R. Gerald McMurtry, present director of the Lincoln National Life Foundation at Fort Wayne, Indiana, both gave liberally of their time and knowledge, as did their secretary, Margaret Moellering.

Stefan Lorant, noted authority on Lincoln photographs, furnished comments on several Lincoln pictures, and the late Professor Robert Taft, expert on the history of photography, replied to technical inquiries.

Particularly significant were the contributions of the photographers who provided negatives or made prints from negatives in the Ostendorf collection. Most of the prints in the book were made by Paul Will and Leo "Bud" Fischer of the Paul Will Studio in Dayton and Paul Agnew of the Agnew Art and Photocopy Service. In Springfield, prints were made by Herb Georg of the Herbert Georg Studio and The Camera Shop. Contributors of prints were also the William E. Hardin studio in Lincoln, Illinois, and the George Eastman House of Rochester, New York. Of great help were the efforts of the Library of Congress and the National Archives photoduplication services.

Most especially the authors wish to thank the secretaries who worked tirelessly on the manuscript. Catherine S. Unold and June Baxter typed portions of the preliminary draft, and Roselle S. Morse and June Keller typed much of the early and final draft. Far more than the work usually allotted to a secretary was accomplished by Judith Irby, who survived long hours of dictation and offered many helpful comments on the organization of the book; and Diane Brooks, who not only aided in the typing but read the manuscript with much critical ability and suggested valuable improvements. Particularly the authors wish to thank Doris H. Hamilton, who helped to outline the volume and contributed many important suggestions, and Rita Ostendorf, whose patience and praise helped to make this a better book.

BIBLIOGRAPHY OF LINCOLN PHOTOGRAPH BOOKS

Lorant, Stefan. *Lincoln, His Life in Photographs*. New York, 1941.

———. *Lincoln, a Picture Story of His Life*. New York, 1952. (Revised and enlarged ed., New York, 1957).

Meserve, Frederick Hill. *Lincolniana: Historical Portraits and Views, Printed Directly from Original Negatives*. New York, 1915. Limited to sixteen copies.

———. *The Photographs of Abraham Lincoln*. New York, 1911. Limited to 102 copies. (Contains 100 photographs.)

———. *Ibid. Supplement No. 1* (Numbers 101–108). New York, 1917.

———. *Ibid. Supplement No. 2* (Numbers 109–16). New York, 1928.

———. *Ibid. Supplement No. 3* (Numbers 117–24). New York, 1952.

———. *Ibid. Supplement No. 4* (Numbers 125–30). New York, 1955.

———, and Carl Sandburg. *The Photographs of Abraham Lincoln*. New York, 1944.

Miller, Francis Trevelyan. *Portrait Life of Lincoln*. New York and Chicago, 1910.

Rogers, Agnes. *Abraham Lincoln, a Biography in Pictures*. Boston, 1939.

Wilson, Rufus Rockwell. *Lincoln in Portraiture*. New York, 1935. Limited to 650 copies.

INDEX

Pearson, T. P. (Macomb, Ill., photographer): 285; photograph by, 17, 264, 360
Pennybacker, Mary Elizabeth Lincoln (daughter of Col. Abraham Lincoln): photograph of, 320
Peoria Star, The: 285
Philadelphia, Pa.: 72, 74, 75
Philadelphia Enquirer: 184
Philp & Solomons (Washington): 149, 230, 278, 282
Photography: daguerreotype, 12, 44; ambrotype, 14; tintype, 27; carte-de-visite, 37; multiple lens, 79, 83; stereoscopic, 81; Scott-Archer wet-plate process, 122; techniques of, 124, 131, 140; Brady method of copying, 165; types of, 356
Piatt, Donn: 61
Pinkerton, Allan: 107; in Antietam photograph, 108, 109
Poore, Benjamin Perley: 115
Porter, Gen. Fitz-John: in Antietam photographs, 107, 110
Porter, Samuel: 133
Profile portraits: comparison of, 104–105
Putnam, Maj. George Haven: 57

Randolph Hotel, Macomb, Ill.: 285
Rankin, Henry B.: photograph of, 343
Read, Judge John M.: 62
Redpath, James: 345
Reeves: in Antietam photograph, 110
Republican Convention (Decatur, 1860): 40
Ridgeway, Anna: 230
Rietveld, Ronald: 235
Richards, F. DeBourg (Philadelphia photographer): photographs by, 72–75, 374
Rindlaub, Martin P. S.: 19
Rocher, H. (Chicago photographer): photographs by, 312, 313

Roll, Frank: 33
Roll, John E.: 33; photograph of, 338
Ross, Gilbert L.: 50
Russell, Sir William: 43, 114
Rutledge, Ann: 332, 333
Rutledge, Mary Ann: photograph of, 332
Rutledge, James: 332

Sacket, Col. Delos B.: photograph of, 107
Saint Gaudens, Augustus: 233
Sand Bar case: 64
Sartain, William: engraving by, 274
Saturday Evening Post, The: 294
Schenck, Maj. Gen. Robert C.: photograph of, 159
Schneider, George: 19
Schwartz, Stephen G.: 255
Schwarz, Carl: 354
Seaver, Benjamin F.: 191
Seavy, William (Canton, Ill., photographer): 31; photograph by, 53, 367
Sellers, Coleman: 102
Seward, William H. (secretary of state): photograph of, 350
"Shawl" photograph (spurious): 291
Shepherd, N. H. (Springfield photographer): photographs by, 4, 5, 246, 298, 355, 359
Shields, Gen. James T.: photograph of, 346
Short, James: photograph of, 333
Slade, William (Lincoln's valet): photograph of, 345
Smith, Caleb B. (secretary of the interior): photograph of, 353
Smith, Clark Moulton (Lincoln's brother-in-law): photograph of, 322
Smith, Mrs. Clark Moulton (Ann Todd, sister of Mary Todd Lincoln): photograph of, 322

Lincoln in Photographs has been a project requiring many months of planning before its appearance in final book form. Placement of type on the pages was carefully planned before composition so as to relate each passage to the appropriate photograph and to the book as a whole. After the final positioning of all type matter on the page, each halftone illustration was inserted into its proper space, and the entire book was produced by offset.

UNIVERSITY OF OKLAHOMA PRESS

Norman